The Campus Scientist

Daniel Edmunds Jr

Dedication

I would like to dedicate this book to my father, Daniel Edmunds Sr.

I have always said that worse things have happened to better people, but I never meant that to

you.

About the Author

Once climbed the empire state building, beat up the giant monkey Kong at the top, spit down on Godzilla and defeated Zeus 2 of 3 times in badminton. Also has collected the infinity gauntlet, mastered ultra instinct, and plans to become a pirate in the near future. I shot a hole-in-one on my first time golfing, on all eighteen holes, then quit because my caddy didn't like the sport. Finally, with some seriousness, in my early twenty's, I struggled greatly with my mental health. I sought help from doctors and therapists, trying anything to get my mind more stable. I continue to play an active role in maintaining and improving my mental health. I go to therapy, which is something I believe everyone should do! With that, I will make my final statement.

An agnostic view is accepted on the road to enlightenment. So, don't risk your integrity with faith.

Try to have fun with this book, folks!

Acknowledgment

I would like to start with anyone I did not get to in this book. If you are wondering why, you weren't mentioned or why our story didn't make it in, it might have been my only sense of normality, and I hold that dear to my heart.

To my mother, Suzie "Homer" Edmunds. I know you have never liked that I call you by your first name, but hopefully, some people get that I did it as an homage to the Simpsons and really thought of you as my disaster parent who always came through.

To Josh Carion, my best friend, my oldest friend, and camp master. You have made almost every right choice in life, and without your guidance and friendship, you would have had a lot of free time because I've been needy for this past decade. Love you, man.

To Brittany Norris, you sparked a fire in my heart and under my ass! You are a wonderful person, and I am so thankful to have you in my life.

To my little brother Chris Edmunds, it's been one hell of a ride! Remember that time you "stole" my car? Good times, man. I love you, brother.

To Jordan Laidlaw, or as I know you, Dobby, a decent worker, better chef, and great friend.

I would also like to thank my writing crew. Thank you for helping me edit my story and breathe life into this book.

Contents

Introduction

In my duties to this novel, I promise to do my utmost to be a good writer, yet it's often the small things that make us great. I hope my views can rise above these shortcomings and offer you something valuable through my words.

When the chaos began is insignificant, but how it concluded is a spectacle worth noting. I firmly believe that the beginning of a book is not as crucial as maintaining the energy and momentum throughout. There will be moments when I am a victim; I was, after all, just a child. There will be instances where I am the hero, as I played a pivotal role in establishing the house of campus science. However, more often than not, I will embody the villain. A solitary figure destined to walk alone, yet planting seeds of hope in others. My actions have left me in an emotional limbo, and now my words must either illuminate the lives of thousands or perish in the melody of my own making.

It is tempting to start with a tale of a sorrowful childhood, blaming every misstep on it and seeking justification for my actions. To be truthful, my childhood was a series of hardships, but it was not what broke me. You could argue that every time I made a joke to deflect from something going wrong as a kid, I was gradually fracturing, but I never truly broke. I knew other kids with even more challenging lives and understood, even at a young age, that parents are far from perfect. Aside from an older brother who subjected me to vicious beatings to the point of unconsciousness and occasional drowning, my parents were a quintessential modern couple of the nineties. My father, a capable Boy Scout who could fix anything, and my mother, a stay-at-home hippie with a heart of gold. I had a pool, dogs, cats, and motorcycles to ride. If my brother hadn't been an abusive drug dealer, I might have become a physicist or pursued something more accessible than writing.

When I was young, I never really knew what I wanted to be. I think that is a common problem many people face. But I did know that no matter what obstacles came my way, I would somehow overcome them. Despite that, I was scared of everything. Above all my fears, my biggest was between myself and God. Both my parents were God-fearing and would often call us godless heathens when we fought. It can be hard to differentiate a phrase from reality, especially between the ages of six and twelve.

I feared God for other reasons, though. I did not like the idea of hell. I remember feeling bad even for the worst criminals when they got in trouble because I thought they didn't understand what they did. Or if they did, what kind of world is this, and what is evil? It took me many years and a lot of reading to feel like I could represent myself against God. When I finally reached that point, I came across a saying: "Why worship a god that punishes you?"

For all that I was, or the world is, I realized we are all the same. Just energy reflecting from sunlight, trying to avoid the darkness. Now, as I sit down to write this novel, I am filled with a sense of purpose. This is not just a story about my life; it is a story about the human condition, about how we navigate the complexities of existence, finding light in the darkest of places. It is a story of love and loss, pain and redemption, and the enduring power of the human spirit.

I do not claim to have all the answers. I am merely a traveler on this journey, seeking to understand the world and my place in it. Through my words, I hope to offer you a glimpse into the heart of our shared humanity, a reminder that we are all connected by the threads of our experiences. As you embark on this journey with me, I ask for your patience and understanding. There will be moments of joy and sorrow, of triumph and defeat. But through it all, I hope to offer you a sense of hope, a belief in the possibility of redemption and the enduring power of love – through writing.

Since I brought it up, you are probably wondering what broke me or made me a writer—call it what you will. Well, of course, it was a woman. I promise the circumstances were over my head and out of my control. What I am going to say is that love and trust are very different things. When you love someone, you do what is best for them. When you trust someone, you do what is best for yourself. I don't want to be the villain of this story or any story. Unfortunately, I think the world needs a proper supervillain.

So, in the name of villainy, fun, chaos, and destruction, I introduce the story of the Campus Scientist to you.

May the darkness avoid my path. Amen.

Chapter 1

The story has officially begun, and I can present the real me to you.

First, picture this: it is my senior year of high school. I am juggling relationships with five different women and having casual encounters with even more. My friends idolize me, thinking I am some demigod. Life is rolling smoothly. I've got an overpaid delivery job at a local pizza place, living comfortably in my parent's basement, and even have a hammock in my room. My plan is to attend I.U.P. after graduation.

But there is a twist in the tale – let's rewind a bit.

I wasn't always this senior with a car, money, good looks, and social status. Back in the day, I was part of a group of misfits. We were the kids who threw parties but stayed sober, opting for bonfires and Roman candle battles over alcohol. We spent our time playing video games, waiting for the day we would finally get our hands on some liquor. We were a tight-knit group, and I loved them dearly. Now, let's get back to the tale.

Have you ever felt lost in a familiar place? That's how I felt every time I walked past the art section in high school. My mother was an excellent artist, talented at drawing and wood-burning, but I could barely draw stick figures. Art always resonated with me because it felt like a reflection of my own existence – often overlooked and unnoticed. I'd find myself late to class, captivated by the drawings my peers created. As a smart kid, I should have known this was the beginning of my horror story.

One day, as I was passing by, a particular drawing caught my eye. It depicted a man opening the daylight sky to reveal the night stars. There was something comforting about it, something that resonated deeply within me. I decided to offer the artist twenty bucks for it. The artist was a popular kid in school, well-liked, and not known for being a jerk to the guys in school. I knew where his locker was, so I approached him. But as I did, I saw him with a girl who looked like a goddess. I had seen her before but never noticed the way her eyes sparkled. She outshone any piece of art. Scientists say our eyes are made of stardust, and this girl seemed to prove it true. I fell for her instantly, but he was one of the most popular kids in school, and I was just a dishwasher – all good things in their own time.

In my case, it was wrong. Love is strange—it can crush you or lift you, change your perspective, make you fester, and make you emotionally unavailable even from afar. I suppose I hoped for the best.

Her name was Julie, and I remembered her from a history class in 9th grade. I had a crush on her back then and even ended up in an accidental picture with her in the yearbook. I was raising my hand, and she sat beside me, looking bored. As messed up as it sounds, I thought if we ever got together, she'd think this was cute.

Good intentions and positive thoughts, right?

But seeing her with him, the love in her eyes didn't make me honorable—it turned me into the very type of scum she was enduring with that guy.

I knew about the pain he caused her, the embarrassment, and the loss of friends. I was always listening. If I were a better man, I would have torn him apart limb by limb. Unfortunately, she would have pieced him back together and loved him even more.

Chapter 2

But Julie wasn't the only girl I showed interest in – hell no.

I dated other women, sometimes getting semi-serious, but I was never able to reproduce the feelings I had for Julie.

That was until I met Cara.

She was the first woman who loved me like I loved her. She had a quirky personality and an athletic build, and she looked at me like I was the center of the universe. For one whole year with her, everything was terrific. The only letdowns were my own—my own fears, my own doubts, my self-sabotaging thoughts. Things were going great with her until it happened. The thing that would ultimately send me spiraling down a path of deceit.

Cara was different from the other girls I had dated. She had this vibrant energy that was contagious, making every moment with her feel special. We would go on long walks, discussing our dreams and fears and sharing secrets we had never told anyone else. She had this ability to make me feel like the most crucial person in the world, and for that, I loved her deeply.

One night, I was with the boys, and as usual, I was on my phone texting Cara and smiling. When they asked why I was so happy, I proudly told them about her. Instead of congratulating me, they chose to belittle her.

"She's not that pretty," one said. Then, like dominos, they all fell. "Yeah, she's not that great," and so on. For what felt like an eternity, I had to sit and listen to my friends tell me why I should be single, messing with someone else, or could do better.

And for whatever reason, I listened to them.

Their words planted seeds of doubt in my mind. I started questioning everything about my relationship with Cara. Was I settling? Could I really do better? These thoughts consumed me, and before long, I found myself talking to a new girl with plans to end things with Cara. I didn't just go out and decide to cheat. I was prompted into it by a beautiful girl. She had a problem jumping the lunch line. I was a junior, and she was a freshman. I worked hard to cut in front of people for three years. When she did it, all I could ask was, "Who the hell are you?"

With a smile, knowing she had already gotten away with it, she said, "Melanie." I treated her like anyone else, telling her to get behind me. She looked up at me with those gorgeous brown eyes and stated, "But I'm hungry." She got me, and I decided to give it a chance, asking her to sit with me and my friends that day at lunch. On our first half-date, she moonwalked for my buddies.

She was instantly in, and now I had two girlfriends.

For the next few weeks, I found myself juggling two relationships. Cara made me feel secure and loved, and Melanie brought excitement and danger into my life. It was thrilling and terrifying at the same time. I felt guilty for betraying Cara, but I was also addicted to the rush that came with sneaking around with Melanie. Why didn't I break it off with Cara? It wasn't that simple.

After about two weeks, I met Melanie's parents. They shot down the idea of their daughter dating a guy who had his own car and lived in a house once raided by the police, making the front page of the newspaper, with guns on the front page and everything. The guns were all legal, by the way. That's a story I should probably tell now so I can move on mentally.

Chapter 3

During the summer of my fifteenth year, I was presented with an exciting situation – a night I will never forget.

My older brother Matthew, a drug dealer, brought a friend over one evening. I forget the dude's name, but he was a trim twenty-one-year-old black guy who looked like he worked out. By all accounts, this guy was high as a kite and carrying a couple of forties with him. He saw me and my friends, Josh, and Ethan, playing Madden. Confidently, he said, "Which one of you bitches think you can beat me at this game?"

At that, Josh just handed me the controller. You see, Madden was the game I was famously known for being good at among my friends.

The game was the Tennessee Titans vs. the Pittsburgh Steelers. I was the Steelers, of course…REPRESENT! He chose the Titans because Vince Young was a fast quarterback. Unfortunately, the dude didn't know I knew how to set a spy.

Eventually, I made Vince Young fumble with Troy Polamalu on a blitz. This dude went off, yelling, "Fuck this shit, I'm going to beat your ass." My friends and I looked at each other and proposed a friendly boxing match instead. He wasn't thrilled, but he took the offer.

In two out of the three rounds, I knocked this dude out. We never got to round three because, after the first two

K.O.s, he got so angry that he threw his gloves off and said, "Nah, now it's fucking real! Out back, now."

We all went out back, except Matthew, who was too busy making himself a sandwich to watch over my possible impending doom. It was three-on-one if anything went sideways, which it would for one of us. The dude said, "Watch your knee, watch your knee." I punched him three times in the face, threw him to the ground, got on top of him, and said, "Tap before I kill you," to which he tapped. Laughing, he got up and said, "You boys are a bunch of hard-asses, aren't you? I like that."

After that, we all went in and had our first sips of a forty-ounce. We chilled the rest of the night, listening to war stories of the drug trade. When he finally left around 4 a.m., he looked at us and said, "I'll be back at 8 a.m. to murder you punk bitches," as serious as anyone's ever threatened me.

My friends and I stayed up the rest of the night until at least 9 a.m., with his threat looming heavily over us. I was agitated about the situation, to say the least, and Matthew knew it! Matthew loved messing with me, and this gave him a golden opportunity. After that went down, he would say shit like, "You're in for it; that dude's cartel level," or "He's going to come for you one day." Because of these circumstances, I am afraid of the dark to this day. Having a mortal enemy after me was a big deal. I mean, I did have a nemesis in school, but that's possibly a story for later.

Nevertheless, I now had enemies. I think it was about two months later that our house was raided by the police. I never actually knew much about my brother's drug empire. I didn't know what level dealer he was, but through the grapevine, I heard he and a few friends ran the tri-county area.

But, because of the night my house got raided, I hated cops more than him or drug dealers. I still do. The reason is simple, really.

When cops kick in the front door of your home, it's wild how much it sounds like the cartel. My bedroom was in the basement of our home, directly under the living room and kitchen, and my room was immediately at the bottom of the basement stairs. The house being made of wood allowed me to hear when anyone was moving around upstairs or coming down the stairs. That night, I could hear every footstep coming into our house. You get really tense when you count about thirty human beings walking through the kitchen and stomping down the basement stairs. Those stupid fuckers didn't even announce that they were the police. When they got to the bottom of the stairs, they simply kicked open my bedroom door with guns trained on a fourteen-year-old. The fucking door was unlocked—they didn't have to kick it in.

At first, I thought, oh, thank God, it's the cops, not the cartel. But boy, was I wrong. You see, the cartel just puts a bullet in you. They don't trash the house, go through naked photos of your mom from the eighties, and leave you in your underwear while they do it like the police did that night. The police were only there for weed, and I swear they had enough police officers there for Jeffrey Dahmer. After that incident, my reputation with the parental community went to shit.

That's why Melanie's parents disapproved of her having a relationship with me, but Melanie was a rebel. Tough as nails and more intelligent than the average bear, we found ways to make it work, but I found myself empty, which restrained me from dating her properly. I couldn't take her to dinner or an amusement park. So, we found ourselves sneaking around. Cara didn't deserve any of this; it wasn't fair to her. I enjoyed the idea of normality with her, and she was beautiful in my eyes. Why wasn't that enough?

Throughout my teenage years, I had a strong supporting cast. We quickly went from guys with nothing to men with jobs and cars—at least the ones who wanted something out of this world. I hate to say it was my job to meet women for the group and bring them to parties, but we all did it. I didn't do drugs, though; I swore that off, and it lasted until I was eighteen when I started drinking and smoking weed.

I swear it was because of the women.

Chapter 4

Before we begin this chapter, I want to remind readers that life moves on, regardless of challenges. Each day brings new opportunities and experiences, pushing you forward even when you feel stuck. Difficult moments shape your tenacity and strength. The world continues to turn, seasons change, and time heals wounds. People come and go, but your journey remains uniquely yours. The same happened to me.

As I progressed in high school, I decided to take a fifth math class, even though only four math credits were required. I wanted to soak up as much knowledge as possible for college and future challenges. Honestly, I felt out of my depth. Unexpectedly, the teacher was so impressed with my determination that she let me copy the girl's paper next to me. That girl was Molly.

Molly and I had been friends since middle school, always supporting each other. At the time, I had a job, but Molly mentioned how I could make double the money delivering pizza for Fox's. It seemed tempting, so I decided to give it a shot.

I turned in my application that day, hungry for more money. In hindsight, I should have known shit wasn't going to go well for me after seeing that giant menacing Fox winking down at me when I walked into the pizza shop. But having two girlfriends was getting expensive, and if there's one thing I've learned, it's that relationships are costly both financially and emotionally. That's why I've had a job since I was thirteen. At this point, I was sixteen, and I had my driver's license for a few months. Luckily, I got the job!

On my first day at the pizza shop, I walked in and saw her. It was Julie, looking beautiful despite being covered in pizza grease, sweat, and flour. Suddenly, all my girl problems seemed insignificant. Right then, I decided I was going to do what I wanted to do until she liked me. Something changed in me that day; I would never be the same. I didn't even know her yet, but I was in love.

Looking back, maybe I was at the edge of insanity, abandoning all rational thinking. Why would this girl, who I knew had dated a cheater, want another one? It seemed like it would take heaven and hell colliding for us to end up together, so I tried to push it to the back of my mind.

I felt wholly cooked. She had just gotten out of a relationship with a guy who cheated on her repeatedly, and here I was, juggling two girlfriends. I was so screwed, you know? But at that moment, I decided that I might as well just do whatever I wanted because there was no redeeming quality I could pull in to save myself right then. I was in too deep, so why not embrace the madness?

So many people drifted in and out of that pizza shop. If you're not mentioned, you probably worked the morning shift (looking at you, Kaylee) or were just passing through on your way to college. I struggled at my job for the first six months, and it was embarrassing. I messed up a lot of deliveries. Once, I accidentally threw a pizza on my roof because I saw a woman come out of her house waving a shotgun, ready to attack me. I fled the scene, losing the pizza as it slipped from the top of my car. It's frustrating when people don't answer their phones after placing an order. Like, if you ordered pizza, why would you ignore your phone?

I ended up leaving that pizza on the road because I sped away quickly, trying to avoid the potential gunfire. When I finally found the correct customers, and they asked me what had happened to their pizza, I shrugged my shoulders and said, "I don't know what happened to it; I'm just happy to be alive!" They started complaining about the missing pizza, but no one believed my story until someone found my delivery bag lying on the side of the road.

During this time, the most I said to Julie was when she made a mistake, and one of the managers started freaking out about it. When he asked me about it, I could only say, "It was Julie." He then asked why I was not mad at her since her mistake had messed up my delivery. I simply responded, "Julie hardly makes mistakes." As I turned and walked away, I could feel her eyes beaming at me. It took six months, but finally, I had my moment.

At the pizza shop, there were four drivers, all of whom were managers except for me, which automatically made them think I was stupid. Each one of those drivers had their own quirks and flaws: there was a stoner, a weird uncle, the golden goose, and, of course, me. The stoner happened to know my older brother. They were close friends – to the point that whenever my brother ordered food, he would pay this stoner driver in weed. Since they were good friends, the stoner thought I was a rat, so he would not talk to me at all.

He thought I was just some snitch for telling my parents about Matthew's weed business, but I did it because I suspected he was doing heroin. I knew weed was okay, but still—I was just a kid! I smoke weed now, but back then, I had to tell on him. My parents understood. If I told them about Matthew, they would take it from me and handle it themselves. If they found it while going through his stuff, they would have to confront him, and I did not want that. I always felt like I was just giving them a heads-up so they could deal with it.

The stoner was a real piece of work. On my first night driving, he warned me not to stare at the map when the boss was around and to avoid using my GPS. Apparently, staring at the map made the boss nervous, while using the GPS made him mad. That was a tough spot to be in, but I figured it was better to deal with the boss's anger than risk the stoner's wrath. Then there was the weird uncle, who constantly reminded me that there are four ways to do things: the right way, the wrong way, the owner's way, and his way. I thought that was just straight-up nonsense. We were just cutting up pizza—there's really just one way to do it. He was the owner's uncle, which is why we called him Uncle. He definitely took a lot of liberties at work.

He was also very creepy. For instance, he once grabbed Julie by the wrist to tell her to leave, and she snapped at him and got his ass fired. She could be fierce! If he had put his hands on her while I was there, I would've had to step in—at least, I think I would have. But the Golden Goose was different. A genuine reformed player, he was an excellent ol' boy who wouldn't steal from the owner, did his job well, and always pitched in when things went south. He had his nipples pierced but never actually wore the rings. He was the only one who would help the cooks on the right side of the kitchen, pulling out and stretching the dough. He had been a delivery driver for so long that he had memorized over 700 roads within a ten-mile radius. The guy was a friggin' genius!

The pizza shop was definitely an experience. One of the most comical parts was when the boxes or "coconuts," as we called them in the shop, would inadvertently come tumbling down on you occasionally when getting one down from the shelf. The "coconuts" had fallen on the Golden Goose's head more than once in front of a crowd. It was just another joke, and he took it like a champ. As for me, it only happened once. The girl who witnessed it was on a date. When she saw them come crashing down on me, she turned her head and laughed uncontrollably into her date's shoulder.

When the boxes fall, it creates such a mess and makes you look ridiculous! Not to mention all the extra work you have to do to pick them up afterward. It sucks. You are standing there, cleaning up the mess while everyone else laughs! It's hard to shake off the feeling of embarrassment. But my life was full of moments like this. Mistakes, quirks, and mishaps that made me a laughingstock and the villain of my own story…

Chapter 5

Throughout my story, I have no intention of sugarcoating anything or trying to soften the blow. I believed the impact would land on me, and I am more than willing to take it. You may ask, why? Well, let's just say I feel like I deserved it…

At that time, since infidelity was my middle name, I did not just have two girlfriends. I might have had a third one as well, judging by how active I was in the opposite-sex category.

Who was my third girlfriend, you ask? Honestly, I have no idea. If I had to guess, it would likely be my pseudo-legendary girlfriend, Samantha—the poor girl in an affluent school filled with bangers. She was different and rolled with friends who made me look like a total pimp. There was Crystal, Amber, and Chloe. I loved those nutty girls, even after they broke into my Facebook and exposed some sexting between us.

When it comes to text messages, there's a whole story involved. I started sexting with Crystal, but I had no idea in reality. I was sexting with all the girls in the group. They were taking turns laughing at me and eventually ended up hacking into my Facebook page to post all those messages online.

The way I found out was ridiculous. I got a call from Maddison from work, and she said, "I think someone hacked into your Facebook." I looked, and there it was—a bunch of sexting posts. I immediately called Samantha, Crystal, and Amber. When they answered the phone, I yelled, "I know you girls did this," and they all giggled in the background.

I pleaded with them. "I have coworkers who see this stuff!" They just laughed and said, "Oh, so the girl you like works with you?" I thought, "Dammit, you really got me this time!"

The only reason I point to Samantha as my girlfriend over any of the others is that she got me into the most trouble. There was always something crazy happening when I was with her, and those adventures often had me questioning my choices (and my sanity).

One time, Samantha and I were coming home from the mall. I was behind the wheel, but she was giving the directions, and somehow, we ended up in West Virginia. I didn't yell at her or anything like that, but I should have seen it coming. She was just giving directions like a little kid in the backseat heading to preschool, saying things like, "Oh, just get on this ramp; that'll take you there." Meanwhile, I'm looking at the signs that say, "Wheeling, West Virginia, 10 miles." But, despite all the trouble that caused me, I wasn't mad at her. How could I be?

Samantha was always saying some ridiculous stuff like, "Danny, they're going to rape us here, come get us." And when I would arrive, armed with a baseball bat, she and her friends would just come out and say, "Danny, we needed you to take us to this party," and I would just shake my head, thinking, "You girls..."

One time, Samantha called me up and said, "Danny, come to this party." When I showed up, I was shocked to find that this party had around eighty guys, plus my friends and those five girls, the ones we knew, plus this girl named Gia, who was just the person hosting the party. The guys from her school were causing chaos, smashing chairs, and breaking vases, while my friends and I were trying to clean up the mess.

Sometimes, during the night, Samantha's sister gets completely drunk. As a result, Samantha turned to me and said, "Hey, Danny, can you take her upstairs to bed, please?"

I looked around and thought, "There's no way I'm taking a drunk girl up to a bedroom alone." So, I told my buddy, Aidan, "Hey, come make sure everything goes smoothly."

We went upstairs, and her sister lay down on the bed, but she would not let us leave. So, we just lay there next to her for a few minutes until she started to pass out. Out of nowhere, some dude kicked the door in, making a hole in it, and saw us lying there with her. He went downstairs and rallied the whole squad, then stormed back into the room, flipping on the lights, and waking all three of us up.

I was sitting there, trying to play it cool, talking in a fake British accent like, "Oh, good day, gov!" just trying to get myself out of that situation. We made our way downstairs, and they ganged up on us. They started throwing weighted medicine balls at my buddy, Connor. We lined up to face them. Someone started counting down to start the fight, and when they got to three, we just sprinted out of there like our lives depended on it!

Samantha always swindled me into something crazy. However, there was this one time I got invited as the only guy to go Black Friday shopping with them, and I did feel special—at least at first. That was until I functioned as a human coat rack, reaching for stuff on the top shelves and standing in line, holding all their purchases. I must admit, though, watching those nutty bitches run around the stores made me smile. After they finished their shopping, they started dragging me into different stores throughout the mall, holding items up to my chest and saying, "This is so you!" It made me feel about as special as any woman ever has.

There were definitely moments that made me feel distinct, like when Cara would whip up fresh fruit for me or when Melanie would have my friends pick her up when I couldn't. It was incredible to have my friends like someone I was dating; it made everything feel more connected.

However, even with the bright spots, I was already snowballing downhill, as you can probably tell.

Chapter 6

We enter this world as social beings, with people constantly entering and exiting our lives. One such individual who left an indelible mark on my memory was Kevin.

Kevin, where do I begin? I am well aware of your transgressions, my friend. Allow me to introduce him to everyone. Kevin was a college friend of my girlfriend, Cara. Now, that guy truly infuriated me. Despite having many opportunities to extend a hand of friendship, he chose to remain passive while my world crumbled around me. I resented him for it because he was privy to the situation. We had worked together for three years, and we were friends, or so I thought.

Then, there were others mocking me for various reasons. They would wager twenty dollars that I would reconcile with Cara after our breakup like it was a fucking game.

Kevin was also dating Natalie, who worked at the pizza shop with us and just happened to be Julie's best friend (remember this; it's significant later). Natalie was insufferable! She would make remarks like, "I'd be attracted to Dan if he wasn't so stupid."

Anyway, let's go back to my football days. It was customary for girls to paint players' numbers on their faces as a symbol of support. They would also make bracelets for their favorite players, which the guys would wear on their biceps like some macho fashion statement. Being a backup, I did not receive such treatment—except from Maddison. She crafted a bracelet for me, which I wore on my wrist like an average person, not a wannabe Hulk.

Maddison was so sweet about it! She would always catch the guys disparaging my long hair or attire—typical high school nonsense. One day, while wearing her bracelet on my wrist as usual, Maddison rushed up, grabbed my arm, yanked the bracelet up to my bicep, and proudly displayed it. I turned to find the guys pointing and laughing, and I remember thinking that if I didn't have to play second string behind my nemesis, the coach's son, I wouldn't be in this ridiculous predicament.

But hey, I was still someone's favorite despite being a second-stringer. Maddison was a kind soul. I hope life has treated you well, Maddison!

Then there were the young hires: Molly's little brother Justin, Maddison's little brother, who was also named Justin, and Jackson. Molly's Justin despised gym class. He was quite a character. He was not what I would call emo per se, but he had the hair and skater attire down to a science. The guy rarely even brought his gym clothes to change into! The only class he might have ever failed was gym, simply for not changing. He would always approach me, saying, "I don't want to be anything but the goalie because I don't want to run around and get sweaty." so I would assign him as the goalie to minimize his effort. We would play a game called

"That's my goalie," where I would essentially take out anyone who approached him too closely.

I will never forget he was at the pizza shop the day I was tackled and put in handcuffs. There he was, working, not even glancing my way, yet it was evident he was upset about everything I was going through. Despite that, he was a good kid.

Maddison's Justin, on the other hand, was more conventional than the others, just trying to fit in while knowing the whole world was trying to pursue his aerobics side-hustle sister. Poor kid had it rough, but he handled it admirably.

Meanwhile, Jackson was a bit of an idiot but still a good kid. I did not mind the younger generation—the kids that came after us. They had their quirks, but they were okay.

Then there were Serena and Janey. Janey was a bubbly, energetic girl. Once, when I didn't have a ball on the Christmas tree with my name on it, she went to the Giant Eagle next door, swiped one of their ornaments, and returned to write my name on it. I cautioned, "I think that's going to get us in trouble." But she just laughed it off, saying, "They're more concerned about people stealing soda!"

She was always incredibly kind to me. There were many instances when I was so busy running back and forth that she made food for me! She was always doing stuff like that for me! Indeed, she was just the most excellent person!

Serena, on the other hand, had her own special kind of loveliness. She had gorgeous hair and those alluring eyes that could weaken anyone's knees.

I ended up taking Serena to prom because one day, she approached me with a picture she wanted to show me. She was dating a guy who was 6'8", and in the photo, he had his arm around another girl. I thought, "If he's showing you this, what a complete jerk!"

I mean, I know what a fuckboy looks like, and he was definitely one. If he is sending you pictures with other girls instead of a cute selfie, he's clearly not even trying. Just a total douchebag attempting to grab attention before prom without any intention of actually showing up.

As I suspected, a week before prom, he dumped her. All week, I was running around thinking, "I'd love to be a proxy because I'm a dipshit," and then she asked me to accompany her, so I did. Let's just say… damn. That guy who ditched her really missed out! Sadly, Serena passed away in a car accident just five years ago. It is still a problematic memory to process.

Now, I've reached the part I've been dreading – explaining everything I worked with. Writing this feels unfair since I had both negative and positive experiences with everyone—except Erin. Seriously, Erin messed up more delivery order slips for me than anyone else. So, Erin, if you're reading this, I hope you find your tires slashed. If you think I am a douchebag for calling out a woman like that, hear me out, please. That girl botched 90 percent of the orders she touched—not just mine, but everyone's.

There was this one time an order came in for a delivery to High Street. Well, there are two High Streets within our delivery radius – one in Shellsburg and the other in Fairfield. Erin had initially written down Shellsburg on the slip but then crossed it out. When I saw that, I thought, "Oh, it must be the one in Fairfield." So, I took the order and drove to Fairfield, and of course, the house numbers eventually ended up showing no sign of my delivery address. You know how it goes. I end up having to drive all the way to Shellsburg, get berated by a customer, and then return to face my boss's wrath. I just remember staring at her, thinking, "You caused all this!" And she's just like, "Oh well," totally unfazed. Classic Erin.

And to top it all off, she was a ginger. I think that just left a bad taste in my mouth for gingers in general after my experiences with her. It was also odd because my boss was this 35-year-old guy who only hired young women and me. What a setup!

I believe I cannot mention the people who left a mark on my memory without mentioning Gerald, Molly's older brother. He deserves recognition for helping me get hired at that pizza shop.

Speaking of which, when I went in for my interview, they started asking me math questions, like, "If the cash register breaks, what do you do?" I replied, "Uh, I pull out my phone and do the math that way." They looked at me incredulously and said, "No, you have to do the math in your head."

I just stared at them and said, "Oh, you mean my phone's broken too? What kind of day is this?" Honestly, I couldn't believe they expected me to do math without my trusty calculator!

But Gerald... you deflected so much attention from my mistakes by being comic relief. For example, when Erin messed up and it became my fault, you would say, "Well, considering the situation, he made good time." Bro, every time you said that, in my head, I called you "Three Point Gerald." Fucking legend.

As I mentioned, I only worked with attractive girls, and I think that kind of made Julie feel average. It was 2009, so let's be honest: females our age didn't typically have jobs. Cara had one, but I had loved her for a year and a half before being shamed into retreating. Julie was intelligent and hardworking. She was even a cheerleader in 9th grade, but that's her story to share if she chooses. I sensed that she was ready to move on from high school, but I think most of us were.

Julie was like a source of inspiration for me. I never thought I'd have the courage to take a shot, but here I am, going for it, even though it feels like taking a full court shot when I can barely reach the basket. In class, I could just crack a joke or read a book to get her attention, but at work? That was a whole different ball game. It's all or nothing. You either excel, or you're out. Julie was extremely popular, and after what transpired with her ex-boyfriend, I think she just felt utterly crushed. I had a plan, though, and it was not a good one. You know what I mean?

So, here's the thing. I was so terrible at my job that, at one point, I seriously thought if my boss fired me in front of Julie, it would destroy me. But I had this crazy idea. I'd walk right up to Julie and pour my heart out—tell her everything, how I'd loved her since I first saw her. Then, I'd turn around, punch my boss in the face, and walk out with both middle fingers in the air, telling everyone to go fuck themselves.

To my 16-year-old self, it was the ultimate fantasy, like a double thrill in the span of two minutes.

My job was challenging. It wasn't just a production line grind; it was before perfect GPS and reliable maps were commonplace. People would scribble their addresses on black mailboxes with black crayons—not exactly helpful, right? I've been cussed at, chased by dogs, and even tipped with weed or alcohol. The weed? It's not the worst thing in the world. But alcohol? Seriously? I'm underage—I can't even drink it!

Chapter 7

Life keeps moving forward, so this book will progress as well. Now, I want to share a bit about the last two girls I dated in high school – Erin and Amy.

I met Emma in class and Amy at the mall. I would love to say I learned something valuable from each of these women, but the truth is, it was 2011, and I was not looking to settle down. I felt invincible, and even if everything fell apart, I figured I would at least get some closure and move on to college. But fuck everyone except yourself, right? I wish I had actually made that choice.

Firstly, when it came to Emma – she was like a best friend.

Emma was different from Amy—she did not bring the same kind of drama. Amy always seemed to attract chaos, while Emma was much more straightforward. She was a farm girl who simply wanted peace in her life despite being drawn to someone like me, who was anything but calm.

Emma and I met in Spanish class. I was terrible at Spanish, but she was not about to do my homework for me, especially with our strict teacher. Somehow, I still managed to get a C in that class. We started spending more time around each other, and things just seemed to click between us.

Our relationship began in a strange yet fascinating way. When I was 18, her friend needed the Plan B pill, and Emma approached me, saying, "Will you get it for my friend?" I, never one to refuse a pretty girl, said, "Sure, you both can come along."

So that's how I ended up buying Plan B for some 17-year-old girl. This resulted in Emma talking to me more and more – to the point where we exchanged numbers and communicated even more frequently. That's how we became friends, and our friendship blossomed into something more. She became my confidant. I started confiding in her about all the women I was seeing and the mental toll it was taking on me. It was almost like she became my therapist.

When it came to Amy, she was the only girl who wanted to date me because she thought I was a 'bad boy.' Other than that, she saw no purpose in me or my life and just wanted to fulfill her fantasy of dating a 'bad boy.' I saw her maybe once a month.

**The mall is such a simple place. It's where I met girls with my friends all the time. You can approach any girl and literally be whoever you want to be! Have you ever heard Kenny Chesney's song, "Out Last Night"? Well, that was me! I was a doctor, a lawyer, a senator's son, Brad Pitt's brother, or a man on the run – literally anything that would intrigue them! That's who I was at the mall, and it is actually how I met Amy. It's kind of a funny story. I told her I was going to college to study trigonometry and become a world-renowned physicist. But in reality, I didn't have any idea what I was going to do with my life. I was just enjoying my youth. Amy was one of those girls who lacked luster, or maybe I was just getting burnt out at this point. I guess you could say that not every encounter comes with a lesson, you know? Not every woman you date teaches you something meaningful. That was kind of my hindrance with Amy. It felt like we were just going through the motions.

When I would visit her, it was like playing a game. I would walk into her house and see how many lies I could tell. I met her parents and fed them all sorts of nonsense—like how I was going to join the Space Force and work on trigonometry to figure out missile trajectories while the Earth rotated. Crazy stuff, right? But they believed it. Her parents were just happy anyone was dating their daughter, even though she was good-looking and had nothing wrong with her. I guess I seemed like a decent guy—smart and put-together—but in reality, I was just having fun with it.

I remember driving 45 minutes to see her once or twice a month. We would meet in the middle, mess around in the car, and that was it. It was fun but also kind of weird. Her obsession with me felt one-sided.

Looking back, the only interest I have now is that if this book does well, I plan to make amends with every girl I hurt, at least the major ones. However, this doesn't apply to Amy because when she was with me, I found out she was engaged to another man. Ironically enough, I don't condone cheating anymore.

Chapter 8

Life, as I have learned, is shaped by defining moments, often moments that are beyond our control. For years, I thought my story was set in stone by my upbringing and the kind of person I had become. The toxic environment molded me into someone I barely recognize now. But life does not stop in those dark places; it urges us to grow beyond our circumstances.

This turbulent phase, where chaos seemed all-consuming, serves as a reminder that growth is always possible, no matter how deeply our past may root us in pain. The path from darkness to light is never easy, but it's in that journey that we discover our true selves.

Reflecting on my unpleasant experiences and sharing them has made me realize their total negativity and how much better off I am now. They've also shown me that my willingness to turn over a new leaf is something to appreciate, and I'm grateful for the opportunity to do so.

To be honest, I hated the house I grew up in, mainly because of my brother, the abusive and malignant drug dealer. All I wanted was to escape that toxic household he created. I did not think much beyond that—I just wanted out.

I used to brag that I was always 500 steps ahead of everyone else, but the truth is, I was making it all up as I went along. This book may seem chaotic, but it was not part of some grand plan. I never considered what others might have been thinking or planning. I was too busy creating chaos like cotton candy—sweet but ultimately empty. I did not care about the consequences or the mess I left behind. I just wanted to feel in control of something, even if it meant leaving destruction in my wake.

Let's start at the epicenter of this farce and tragedy. I will say it outright—the events leading up to this mess are my business, but the event itself? I had nothing to do with it. At least, that's what my therapist keeps telling me. Who knows, maybe they're right. It is not my place to speculate or dwell on what I cannot control. But there are undeniable truths that carry weight in this story, and I owe it to you to share them. What happened before might not be mine to own, but the fallout is something I cannot ignore, and it's crucial to understanding everything that came after.

I had this friend—at least, I thought he was a friend. We were in class during my senior year, and I had to give a speech about my hero. I chose my father. The details of the speech aren't necessary, but what mattered was how I ended it. I said, "My father made a junior to his name, and I will never fully fill those shoes." I thought it was deep, maybe even worthy of an A+ in a communications class.

As I sat down, David—my "friend"—leaned over and said, "I was named after my cousin Dylan Gregory Grey. His last name used to be Beachley (which, by the way, is Julie's last name), but now it's Grey. Isn't that awesome?"

I stared at him for about five seconds before sitting back down, thinking, what in the actual fuck was that? It was like he twisted my moment into something completely irrelevant and bizarre. I wondered if he even heard a word I said or if he was just waiting to make it about himself.

The teacher was ancient—like 103 years old. If I had thrown David across the room and started wailing on him, there was no one to stop me. It would have been total anarchy.

I thought there was no way he'd say that to me. I had people who would have beaten his head in for it. But instead of reacting, I just walked away.

David and I didn't really hang out that much. We would chat in homeroom, but if I'm being honest, I was usually busy hustling to finish homework or cramming for tests. We came from different cliques, and while David wasn't a bad guy, with him, it was either straight-up honesty or wild, crazy-ass bullshit. I didn't like my odds and didn't really understand why he would make it a point to tell me that, but I decided to believe him. Something seemed off, and I was not about to dig deeper into what could have been a complete lie. I wish I had listened to my gut on this, but I couldn't help myself. That one sentence from him helped to fuel the madness that was to come.

We were 90s kids living in a gray area in society. If you didn't get at least a C in a class that your parents' thought was important—and it was a big deal. Getting a C in physics might slide, but failing English? They would lose it. "You're a fucking idiot—it's the language you speak!" That's just how it was back then. The expectations were all over the place, and we were just trying to navigate through it.

Later, I ran into David at a party, and he wanted to hang out. I declined, thinking that if he already liked me and I started dating Julie, it might be weird if we were already good friends. Maybe it would work out better if I stayed a little more distant for now and then got closer to him later.

I wasn't trying to manipulate him, but I was trying to play it cool. I was figuring out how to navigate the situation, thinking ahead about what might work best in the long run. It wasn't about being sneaky; it was just about being smart, you know?

But that's not how David's story ends...

Chapter 9

David was one of those people who made me pause and think about life—how fucking cruel it could be. When I tell you more about him, you'll understand what I mean.

After high school, everything changed. I took a year of classes at a stay-at-home college—a branch campus of IUP close to home. But before any of that, something happened that changed everything:

David jumped off a bridge.

It was a tragic event, and I will not speculate on the reasons why he chose to end his life. I am going to share my last encounter with him because I feel that it bears weight on the story and everything that followed.

As I said earlier, I knew David from high school. Meeting him was a turning point for me. During freshman year, you deal with seniors beating up on you, and your classmates try to fit in with the older crowds. But by senior year, it clicks. You realize you are all basically the same people on the same level. Everyone starts treating each other better. There is just this unspoken understanding that we're all just trying to make it through this phase of our lives together. Sure, we were bullies to the younger crowd—that's just the pecking order in high school. But with each other, we found a way to connect and go through tough times together. It was a wild ride, but those moments of camaraderie made it all worth it. Our final encounter was when we both went to a party at my friend Ben's house. The parties I would throw were more like intimate get-togethers compared to one of Ben's parties. Ben threw bangers! One time, I counted 50 people at my place, but Ben always had a crowd in the low hundreds. Ben built cabins in the woods with a deep, winding driveway, while all I had were couches, hammocks, and three TVs in a basement with no walls.

Ben had these double doors on his house, so naturally, when I walked into that party, I swung both of those doors open, and surprisingly, the first person I saw was David. He was standing in the middle of the room, arms wide open, ready to greet me.

"Danny Edmunds!" he shouted, and I shot back, "David Duncan! What the fuck do you want?" He just hugged me, all pumped up, and asked, "Do you want to play some fuckin' flip cup?" I jokingly replied, "Is there cocaine at this party? Because if there is, I'm in."

But it turns out there wasn't any coke there; he was just super excited to see me.

We jumped right into the flip cup game, and before long, we were drinking heavily and eventually transitioned into beer pong. It was one of those nights where everything felt carefree, and we were just living in the moment, wholly caught up in the chaos and camaraderie.

I can't give you a lot of details about that night because, honestly, it's hard to remember anything after 12 beers and two joints punch you in the face. But I do remember hanging out with him, the smile on his face, and the laughter we shared. Being on a team with a guy as famous as David made me feel accepted, as if I finally belonged.

It was incredible. This was everything I hoped it would be—meeting new people who welcomed me with open arms, each with their own ideas and stories. Instead of clashing, we connected over our shared experiences, and it felt like we were all part of something bigger.

As I was leaving the party and walking toward my car, David called out, "Oh, you're leaving?" I told him I was getting an Uber, but he could tag along. ((I don't condone the dumb things I did when I was younger. Unfortunately, most of us have done something we look back on and aren't that proud of. Driving while intoxicated is not something anyone should do.))

David asked if he and another buddy he was with could hitch a ride down the road. I didn't mind; I knew the Uber driver. When I dropped them off where they were going, David went to get out of the car but stopped, turned around, and looked me dead in the face, asking me if I wanted to smoke weed with him that weekend. I said no. I have no idea exactly why I said that, but I did. It wasn't that I thought I was better than smoking weed with him; I did it for Julie. I didn't want her to think I was suffocating her by spending too much time with someone I believed was her cousin.

I was like, "Oh, come on, man. Just get away from my car and go enjoy the party." He shrugged and walked away. Then, Tommy, the other guy that was with David, who I didn't like that much—he was kind of a jerk to me back in high school—came up to me.

Even though we were all trying to be friendly that night, he said, "Hey, you should be nicer to David. He's thinking about killing himself."

I was shocked. David Duncan? The guy with the scholarship, a good family, and seemingly everything going well for him? It did not make any sense to me at that moment. There was no way I could believe it.

He was like a pirate sailing under the moonlit sea, mysterious and captivating. If a pirate were a person, that's him. He was a whole adventure wrapped up in one. Why would this kid want to end it all? I couldn't believe it. So, I stayed in my car, frozen, and did nothing.

That was the last interaction I would ever have with David.

The weight of that moment still lingers with me, haunting my thoughts as I reflect on what I could have done differently. It's an agonizing feeling, even after so much time has passed. My mind often projects his face in front of my eyes, making it all the worse.

A week after that interaction, I had double flat foot surgery. Two weeks after that, David took his own life.

I found out about it in a weird way. My friend Ashely texted me and said, "Danny, David is dead." At first, I thought she meant he had gotten into a car accident or something like that. I was like, "Damn, that sucks," but not surprising with some of the crazy shit we got ourselves in to. But then she said something that would make my stomach churn. "Danny, He jumped off of a bridge." I couldn't believe it. It felt like something beyond anyone's imagination.

I didn't attend his funeral because I couldn't stand to see Julie cry. I felt useless, as if I had let their family down. I think everyone feels that way after a tragedy, but somehow, I felt closer to it. I should have gotten out of the car, confronted him, and told him what his death would mean to everyone, for me and Julie. I wanted to scream at him about how insecure I would be for the rest of my life over it. Would I ever get a chance to tell them I'm sorry?

But, regardless of tragedies, life rolled on. I went back to school, made new friends, and continued to work with Julie at the pizza shop. Beneath the surface, though, a storm was brewing. As with any storm, no one saw its true destructive force until it hit land. The weight of David's loss hung heavy over me, and I could feel the pressure building, ready to explode at any moment. Little did I know the aftermath of this tragedy would ripple through my life in ways I couldn't yet imagine.

Chapter 10

I'd love to start this chapter with a simple phrase:

Fuck, the local college's main campus is where it's at. But let's move on.

I made a new friend at college whose name was Connor. We were great together, like Batman and Batman, if you will. Honestly, what's better than two Batman's? That year, I actually managed to keep my grades up, which was a miracle considering the chaos surrounding me. I was all set to move to the main campus the following fall with my buddies Connor, Aidan, and Sean.

Connor was a total war machine, always pumped up and ready to go. Aidan was your classic farm boy, down-to-earth and handy. Then there was Sean, who had a thing for superhero girls. Together, we were an odd but perfect little crew.

When we finally moved into our townhouse on the main campus, it was a three-story building with four rooms. Of course, I ended up with the last pick—stuck in the middle row with no windows. But on the bright side, it was right next to Connor's room, so I guess it felt right after all.

I arrived on a Sunday, with my first class at 10 a.m. the following day. I was ready to tackle it, but the parking lot was a nightmare—infested with people like a damn carnival, but with liquor instead of rides. It was chaotic, and I had no idea how I would navigate that mess. Ultimately, I snuck through the back of a fraternity, and as soon as I walked in, it was like entering a new world. There were titties everywhere—well, not the real deal, but cutouts from magazines. This wasn't the Playboy Mansion, but it was oddly intriguing. I hadn't even been there for three minutes when someone shoved a bottle of pink liquor in my hand and said, "Hold this," before strutting off arm-in-arm with some pretty girl.

I made my way through an archway and plopped down on a couch, taking a sip of the pink liquor I'd just been handed. As I sat there, watching a wild beer pong match unfold, I couldn't help but feel a weird sense of familiarity. It was like being at home, but instead of the usual chaos, about fifteen thousand people were partying all at once.

While sipping my pink concoction, I noticed a blonde chick sitting next to me on the couch. Honestly, she wasn't all that great-looking, but by that point, with enough of that pink shit in my system, all the girls started to look good. It was all part of the crazy experience, and I was just trying to soak it all in.

As we were making out on the couch, I suddenly felt this weird sensation of someone staring at me. It was like there were eyes watching me from everywhere in the room. Honestly, it felt like I was being scrutinized from every angle—like the walls were whispering secrets.

While I was kissing this girl, I had this strange revelation. For some reason, the eyes of the people around me didn't have nearly the same effect on me as the eyes in the pictures hanging on the wall. It was a bizarre comparison, but those images were oddly captivating.

While lost in the kiss, I turned my head, looking towards the wall. There was a picture frame filled with frat boys, kind of like a school yearbook, with each guy's face and name neatly labeled underneath. And I swear to God, one of those faces met my gaze head-on—Dylan Grey. I couldn't believe it. Here I was, caught up in this wild party, and somehow, a guy I recognized was staring back at me from that frame.

That sent a chill down my spine. I instantly stopped kissing that girl and sat up, looking around the room to get my bearings. I quickly got up, spotting this stunning blonde with piercing blue eyes just staring at me. I thought to myself, "Maybe another night, sweetheart." I walked past her, navigating around the duplex's staircase and heading upstairs. I mean, what worse could be waiting for me up there?

When I finally reached the top of the stairs, I was greeted by Cara's sister's ex-boyfriend, Austin. He was chatting with some girl, and when he saw me, he greeted me with over-the-top enthusiasm. I don't even know why I responded the way that I did. I guess it was some sort of respect for Cara after hearing all the stories she had told me about him because there's no other reason I can think of.

He looked at me and said, "Hey, Danno, what's up, brother?"

So, I shot back with, "Ayeeee, didn't you and Alicia have an abusive relationship?" I gave him some finger guns and walked away. I remember thinking to myself, "This won't have any repercussions," as I walked away.

That night, for maybe the first time in my life, I felt like a social butterfly, flitting around the room and chatting up as many people as I could. I went from running a beer pong table to getting sloshed while talking to pretty women. I was living my best life, soaking up the energy and chaos around me. It was wild and exhilarating, and I had no idea how it would end, but I was ready for whatever came next.

Eventually, the night did come to an end. I stripped down to my underwear and crawled into bed, ready to crash. As I settled in, I saw the alarm clock in my room—it was already 3 a.m. At that point, I really should have just let the alcohol win and passed out, but like a total jackass, I plugged my phone in to charge. It had died earlier in the night, and I hadn't gotten around to charging it until now.

Of course, the fucking thing started vibrating like it was having epileptic seizures. I glanced at the screen and saw messages from three different people lighting up my notifications. Great, that was just what I needed. Now, I had to deal with whatever drama was waiting for me in my inbox.

First up was Cara, who graciously texted me, "I hate you." Then came her sister, April, who had sent a barrage of messages that I was definitely too buzzed to decipher. And, of course, there was Austin—the guy I had just accused of being an abuser right in front of another woman.

Repercussions, right? But honestly, I was in no mood for this shit. I'd had a great night, and I wasn't about to kick off my week with their bullshit.

Austin's text simply read, "Hey, what's up?" I shot back, "Bro, what have you done?" He responded with, "Called you out on your pussy-ass bullshit." Now, being the reasonable man that I am, I could've taken a step back, talked it out, and avoided all this drama. But I was in a new place, and something inside me just didn't want to back down.

With anger boiling in my heart, I typed back, "Walk back down here." I've always believed in keeping my cool and not letting anger fight for me, but that night felt different. It was a weird mix of emotions, and I could almost feel that reckless youth and invincibility coursing through my veins, daring me to embrace the chaos.

Maybe it was all the alcohol, and Adderall I had already downed—or was about to—but I swear, I felt like I was going to win this fight before it even started. I was in what I like to call full sensei mode. After responding to Cara's sister's texts for what felt like an eternity, I decided to wake up my roommates, thinking this was gearing up to be a full-out war.

I popped 20 mg of Adderall, even though Connor was like, "Bro, you're gonna have adrenaline pumping through you, and that shit won't even kick in until after the fight!" But I didn't care. I was so fucking angry at this punk; how dare he ruin my night when I had already messed up his? It took him about fifteen minutes to drive over, and he claimed he even had a surprise for me.

I was ready, though. I had my three roommates with me, plus Tatum and a sleeping Jordan on the couch. Not to mention, there were still a ton of people in the parking lot partying—the same people I'd just been having a blast with. I felt like I had the home-field advantage, and I was pumped.

As he got out of his car and walked over, I turned to Tatum and said, "Let's go." We approached Austin together, and when we reached him, I asked the one simple question that could've settled things right there: "Are you sorry?" He shot back, "Fuck that." I shrugged, throwing my arms up and to the side, saying, "Okay, then."

We put our fists up, and Tatum threw his arm down between us, saying, "Go." I took a moment to size him up, giving it about two seconds to see if he'd throw the first punch. Call it instinct, but I could tell this guy had some training; he looked like he knew what he was doing but had never actually engaged in a real fight while I had a lifetime of experience. I remember Cara had mentioned that he did MMA or wrestling or some shit like that, but from his footing and stance, I could see he was in no position to throw a punch.

Maybe it was just that he was short and stocky, but my reach on him was immaculate. I felt confident in my advantage, and I was ready to put my experience to the test. Everything around me faded away, and it was just me, Austin, and the electric tension in the air. At any rate, I threw the first punch. Austin didn't roll with it or go down when it connected, but I could feel myself pulling through hard on him. I've got to give him props, though—despite everything, he threw a punch back at me. Unfortunately for him, this was sensei mode; this was God mode. I saw it coming and ducked it fast—maybe too fast.

Let's not forget I had double flat foot surgery just about eight weeks before this fight, and the idea that I was fully healed was a joke. So, I ducked under the punch, but my feet gave out on me. Instead of falling, I stumbled, walked right under him, took two steps, and looked up at the moon. We were back-to-back for what felt like an eternity, though I was told after the fight it was only about 5 seconds. I wish I could say that while staring at the stars, I had some master premonition, but what was even better was the calmness I felt at that moment.

That calm was short-lived, though. Austin grabbed my left arm with both hands, bringing me back to reality. I looked down at his grip and thought, "Oh shit." If you don't know much about grappling, just know that it's a bitch to get out of. So, I took two steps back, lept into the air, and managed to loosen his grip while tossing him in the process. I landed and skidded onto my side, but he was quick. Before I was even done sliding, he was back on top of me, ready to continue the fight.

Unfortunately for him, the fight was already over. You see, I was hyper-focused on his soul, and I could tell he was scared. I rolled him onto his right side, leaving my right arm free while he was pinned to the ground. Then I let loose with three haymakers to his face, followed by three sharp jabs to his nose.

After that, I asked him another question that had severe repercussions if answered incorrectly: "Are you done, or are you sorry?" The "sorry" part came with another punch behind it because I hated repeating myself, and I had already asked him this. Luckily for him, he said he was done.

By this point, at least twenty people had gathered around, and as we both stood up, they started chanting for round two. Just as we lined up for another go, Tatum walked up to Austin and said, "Hey man, Danny just kicked your ass." Everyone laughed. Austin smiled and extended his hand for a shake. We shook hands, and he went home. If it had just been two dudes beefing over something trivial, it would've been over right then and there.

But that was far from the end. The next night, an army of people would show up, intent on seeking revenge and taking me down in the streets. But before I dive into that, I want to share how I became this monster in the first place.

Chapter 11

You know, I've heard all this time how wild December 10th, 1992, was. My mom used to swear up and down about one of the worst blizzards she had ever seen. And yep, that's the day I chose to come into this world. You could say I have been dealing with some rough weather since I was born.

Growing up, I went through a lot. Too much, really. But one thing I regret the most is that I was a coward. Not that I didn't have my reasons. You would be scared, too, if you had to share a room with a psycho. Some call that psycho my older brother, Matthew, but for me, he was a walking nightmare.

Take this one time: I was seven years old – yes, only seven. I was casually watching TV and enjoying my cartoons when my parents gave me a choice of going to my grandparents' house for the day or staying home and being babysat by Matthew. What do you think I chose? I opted to chill at home and do my own thing rather than being bored at my old grandparents' house. I chose straight-up violence for myself, but I didn't know it then.

That day, Matthew decided to increase his beatings from bruises with fists to scars with weaponry. It started off as just another day. I was glued to the TV screen when he came to me with buttered bread. He placed it in front of me, but what I noticed was the long, sharp knife in his other hand. He then looked me dead in the eye and informed me, "This is your last meal. You are going to die today."

My options were to die right there or run for my life—what would a seven-year-old have chosen? I was so scared because I knew the cruelty he was capable of. Matthew was six years older than me, making him around thirteen years old at that time. The chances of me getting out of this situation unscathed were minimal. I ran!

He chased me all over the house, swinging the knife at me, coming closer each time to hitting me. Obviously, that fucker had a lot more strength than seven-year-old me. Finally, the inevitable happened: He sliced my right foot—my fucking foot!

Despite that, I didn't stop running. With blood all over the house, I finally managed to get to my bedroom and lock the door, crying and clenching my bloody foot. I had no strength to fight back against that motherfucker. Our bedroom doors weren't made from solid oak, so his one punch broke the door, and there he was, standing right in front of me with that knife, which had my blood on it.

At that moment, when I saw him standing in my bedroom doorway with an evil grin, I stopped crying. I realized it was up to me to save myself. I saw death right in front of me, and I decided not to go down without a fight. I stared that fucking cunt right in the eyes, and he finally knew he had done some real damage. His smile disappeared as he realized he could be in some deep shit. He suddenly had a change of heart, or at least that's what I thought. He bandaged my foot up. And then came his authentic self—this fucker threatened me. He warned that he would finish the job if I ever told our parents.

He got a badge for first aid in scouts, and I learned how to keep a secret.

The beating never stopped; I had become a coward in his presence. My older brother was brutal beyond what words could explain. People always tried to relate their sibling spats to my abuse, saying things like, "Oh, my brother and I would go at it all the time" or "My brother and I fight all the time." Bro, no, that's not what we had. It was him torturing me. I wanted to scream at these people, "Bitch, has your brother ever drowned you in a pool or beaten you with a baseball bat? For fuck's sake, I was six years younger than him!"

I dealt with his brutal beatings for years as I watched him slowly tear our family apart. But Matthew? He couldn't care less. He was selling weed in the early 2000s and making everyone's life a living hell because he didn't give a damn about anyone but himself.

I remember my fifteenth birthday so vividly as if it were yesterday. I had one of my girlfriends coming over. I went into my parents' room to grab some cleaning supplies and fresh sheets. Matthew was in there, monopolizing the TV as usual. Dad wasn't home from work yet, and Mom was out with my grandmother at her doctor's appointment.

So, Matthew, my younger brother Chase, and I were at home. I tried to grab what I needed quickly because walking by Matthew without things going sideways was next to impossible. He yelled, "Stay out of Mom and Dad's closet. Wait for them to get home." I shot back, "I just talked to

Mom, and she said it's fine," which apparently was the code for "Fuck you."

The next thing I knew, he walked over and lightly pushed me. For whatever reason, that push unleashed a rage in me I hadn't known I had. I punched him hard, and he spun around, landing on the bed. He tried to get up, but this was my time, bitch. I kept swinging again and again until his face was smashed and a bloody mess. At one point, I struck him so that his face bounced off the bed, and I caught him on the upswing, delivering a "hammer of God" punch at that exact moment. I only stopped when the walls were splattered with blood.

Now, remember, I was fifteen, and Matthew was in his prime at twenty-one. The fight was far from over. Chase walked in and looked over, trying to understand what had happened, which gave Matthew the distraction he needed. He came at me harder than expected. I can still feel the pain.

We ended up in the bathroom, trading punches and kicks until he ripped off a towel holder and smashed it over my face. Thankfully, it was plastic and hollow, so we both paused for a second, thinking, "Is that it?" Then I took out my old offensive lineman moves and drove him backward out of the room, slamming the door shut and locking it.

Chase and I stood there, backs against the door, waiting for Matthew to come charging through or for a knife to pierce the wood. He was going ballistic in the kitchen, smashing everything like a lion with a thorn in its paw. This mouse was damn proud to have put that thorn there. We called our mom and told her everything. She answered that she would return soon and that we should both stay in the bedroom. It was the longest forty-five minutes of my life. To this day, I almost died on my birthday, so if any girl I have dumped on a holiday or their birthday is reading this, look at this perspective!

When my mom got home, there was blood everywhere: carpet, wall, you name it. She thought I was dead. But surprise, surprise, Mom, I was mostly fine. On the other hand, Matthew had run off to a buddy's place for some first aid.

My birthday was obviously canceled, and just like that, I was punished for finally standing up for myself. The only silver lining was that my dad was prouder of me than he had ever been before. While this old man never forgave violence or laid a hand on us, he also knew when there comes a time when you've got to stand up for yourself.

Growing up in that kind of environment would make anyone jumpy. It was like playing Russian roulette, but all the chambers were loaded with this guy, Matthew. I kept quiet about it at school, though. Whenever someone tried to push me around or talk shit about me, I would laugh it off. If they only knew what I was capable of.

People had heard stories, fights, and scuffs here and there, but I never needed an audience for a brawl. I liked my role as an enforcer rather than a fighter; I had just stood there while someone else made their first move. I didn't have much of a childhood. I got my first job washing dishes at a local diner when I was thirteen. By then, my brother had torn the family apart so much that divorce was on the table, and my dad was busting his ass to save up for the American dream— a fully paid-off divorce. I didn't have much to work with; it was just my birthday and Christmas combined.

Yes, it's a bitch being born in December. I never had clothes bought for me because I was usually given the option to choose between a gaming system or new clothes. That's just not fair to a kid. Naturally, I had to steal clothes from my brother, which, of course, resulted in countless ass-kicking. I once went to school wearing one of his shirts and got clowned all day because it was too small and looked 'girly.' When I got home, Matthew kicked the shit out of me for wearing it. That was when I realized I couldn't have it all—I was going to get smoked in my life. It felt like no one took care of me or gave a damn. If they ever did, it was just artificial, or they were just using me as their backup, those motherfuckers.

Chapter 12

I never really played with puzzles, but life sure gave me plenty to solve. The only trouble was I couldn't start piecing them together until now because so many pieces were missing. My life had become a disorganized mess resulting from a series of uneven and unwanted events that no one in my family was willing to accept.

Here's what happened: I landed my first job thanks to my friend's uncle. It was a haphazard gig, but I was thrilled to take it on. Some under-the-table work was involved, and I got paid the same day. Now, imagine having pride in a job that pays you the same day and at the ripe old age of thirteen. Getting paid daily was my little flex. The money felt like a fortune to me, enough to last a lifetime—or so I thought. But, as it turned out, it wasn't nearly as much as I imagined.

One day, when I was done with work, my friend's uncle was driving me home. The car was quiet, and the window was rolled down. I closed my eyes and let the gentle wind hit me, feeling the breeze growing stronger as the car sped up. When the car slowed, the breeze calmed, and I glanced out the window. What I saw made my heart drop: there was a barrage of cop cars as well as an ambulance lining my driveway. My friend's uncle, seeing the scene in front of him, did not know what to do. He simply dropped me off at the end of my driveway and drove away, leaving me standing there, stunned.

Making my way toward the house, I stumbled past the cops, who didn't say a damn word to me, but their eyes spoke volumes I couldn't quite decode. I walked by the ambulance and heard my mother screaming. I looked into the ambulance, and all I could see was her feet handcuffed to the gurney. I was scared as hell, perplexed, and anxious. All I knew at that moment was that something was seriously fucked up—for all I knew, I was now the man of the house. Things were not the same as they used to be. I walked into the house and saw my dad's face buried in his hands. That's when everything felt like it stopped. The scene was heartbreaking, and my dad's position made me go numb. My body just wasn't cooperating.

There were fifteen cops there, and none of them had a clue what to do when I showed up. They saw a thirteen-year-old boy that was tall for his age, around six feet, and they just assumed I'd handle myself. Another reason I don't trust the police is that they were too busy interrogating my father to even look at me or do anything helpful. So, when I got inside, I ran straight into my dad's arms.

We were both crying. He told me we needed to head to the hospital. My older brother was already out, and my little brother was going to stay with the neighbors. Dad needed someone with him to help him during such times, and that became our thing. Every time Mom would overdose, throw herself out a window, or do something similar, it was me and Dad handling it. My father and I went to the hospital to see my mom. I knew she'd shot herself, but the details were a blur. I had no clue what drove her to this. The whole scenario made my mind spin ten times more than usual. I do specifically remember that not a single cop there that day seemed to have the fucking training on how to handle this situation. Fuck the cops—barbers train longer than you, guys!

I remember being in the hospital, sitting there with my dad, waiting to hear how my mother was doing. My dad had asked if he was able to see Mom when one of the nurses informed him that my mom had yelled, "I don't want Dan Edmunds in this hospital room." My Dad and I share the same name, so when I heard that, all I could think was, "Do you even remember you have a son named Danny?" That was tough.

Eventually, I became so desensitized to Mom's attempts to kill herself that I was more excited about the food we would stop and get on our way home from the hospital. Even as a kid, I knew it was messed up, but I was more eager to be with my dad. I always thought Mom would pull through, so I was messed up about it. No jokes here, just the reality of it.

Did she get better? Yeah, she did. Things improved, though she was still a stressed-out person. She eventually got prescribed the proper medications, and life settled down. We took away all firearms, though we still have guns, but we keep them secured.

Six months passed without my mom, and nobody came out of it unscathed. Not my brothers, not even the psychotic one. Watching my dad spiral into depression, I felt like I had no choice but to take on the responsibility of running the household. They say there's always a woman behind every man's success, but in my case, the woman behind my success was no longer there. After my mother's spiral into such a condition, no one was left to look after my needs. The Simpsons and Family Guy essentially raised me.

Later on, as I grew up, I lost my virginity to a 19-year-old girl in a trailer park on New Year's Eve. That's what set me up for the stellar life of self-hate and misery I have now. And oh, that 19-year-old girl—how are you doing? Lol. Thanks for the dark room, the pounding on the door from your friends threatening death, and the inability to fall in love without it being twisted as hell.

This story has gone in all fucking directions, and I apologize for that, but here's the reason: I'm mentally fucked up, not well, sick—whatever label you want to throw on it—and I don't know what I'm doing. But here's a message I don't want to surprise anyone with: I didn't realize how awful my life was until I lost everything. I lost everything because I let pride and self-entitlement cloud my judgment. In my defense, though, Julie is a stone-cold dick killer, but I stand by my disagreement.

So, where was I? Oh yeah… I just beat that dude's ass and was explaining why I'm so fucked up. Well, what makes me crazy is this lovely combo called "trauma and comedy." Hmph!

I had a lot pent up in me. You'd think by now I'd have learned to act normal, right? Eh! After the fight, Austin texts me and says, "I can't believe I lost!" to which I replied, "Yeah, I felt bad I had to do it."

Who the fuck am I? Why do I keep prodding shit on? The next day went lovely. My 'peaceful' sleep was interrupted by a phone call from none other than Cara. I was groggy enough not to check the caller ID when the phone rang.

"Hello?" I croaked out.

"Hey!" she chirped, all full of life and spunk.

Then, and I'm not making this up, I yelled, "Fuck you! Fuck you! Fuck you! Fuck you!" To which she responded frantically, "Oh! Somebody's got a temper now!" I hung up, feeling mocked, only to see the clock and realize I was late for class.

Later that day, while I was getting dressed, Connor barged in and said, "You are NOT going out tonight!"

It was an order so direct and laced with so much warning that I stared at him. In my usual brilliance, I asked, "Why?"

He gave me a dull look and walked over to the window, yanking open the shades. Outside, there were about seventy-five to one hundred people.

I reacted with a classic O-face and said with a smile, not taking the situation seriously and playing with TNT and Zippo lighters like a fucking firestarter. "Cool! Big party, let's go!"

In response, Connor grabbed me by the shirt collar, pulling me close and locking eyes with me, giving me that 'wait-you-didn't-let-me-finish' look.

"They're outside handing out beers and looking for you by name," he said, his eyes wide, "They're ready to kick your ass. I was supposed to come here and get you, but I put everything on lockdown."

I still didn't take the situation seriously until Connor said: "We're not going out there."

So, when Connor, the weightlifter, Super Saiyan, and muscular dude, said that, something happened. I'll never forget the moment I looked around at Jordan, Tatum, Aidan, Connor, and Sean holding a freshly packed bowl, thinking, "Fuck them, the weeds in here,"

So, we got high and drunk, laughing our asses off at the army of people who showed up to tear me limb from limb. I didn't think about it at the time, but it was the happiest I'd been in a long time. Without a mob out there, I wouldn't have had this chance to enjoy myself. The boys inside the house showed me who my true friends were. It felt like we were on top of the world like we'd just conquered something significant.

The happiness I felt didn't have an apparent reason, but being happy was a victory. I felt like I had unlocked some sort of code for invincibility—the ability to knock someone into such a rage and then walk away still standing tall.

Chapter 13

You know, they say karma's a real thing. And if you're anything like I was back in the day—reckless, thinking the world was your playground—then you've probably already felt her cold, hard slap across the face. Trust me, she doesn't miss it. Never.

You see, I used to think I was untouchable. No consequence too big, no mess too messy. But here's the kicker: life has a funny way of serving up exactly what you deserve, whether you're ready for it or not. And in my case, well, let's just say the universe kept the receipts.

One of the things this book is all about is the moment when everything you've dished out comes back around. The hangovers might fade, but the lessons stick. Buckle up because Karma's about to show you why she's not someone you want to mess with.

That week, I went to school like any other, but it was syllabus week—a time when classes were light and drinking games were heavy. We spent most of our time outside, gathered around the tables from our apartments, just soaking up the college vibe.

We lived in these three-story townhouses. We were in apartment two, and the girls in apartment four were something else. They were kind enough to help us settle into college life, and boy, they showed us the ropes. They introduced us to new people, taught us how to hold our liquor, and even helped with my studies when I was struggling.

I won't sugarcoat it—they were a bunch of no-goods, slutty bitches, but in a weird way, I couldn't have asked for better guides to make us acclimate to the wild ride that was this party school.

My three-part plan was simple: start at IUP Northpointe, transfer to IUP's main campus for a year, and then jump to Pitt to be with my best friend, Ethan. Part of that plan included joining the Delts fraternity, where Ethan was already a brother, so naturally, I had to make that happen.

I decided to go for it and brought Connor along for the ride.

The moment we showed up, we were instantly paired up with bigs and littles—like a built-in family to help you pilot the craziness of college life. My big was known as Rambo, and let's just say he had a serious love affair with my Adderall prescription. But hey, he and the rest of the Delts did everything for Connor and me, from hooking us up with beer and girls to making promises of good grades. It was all part of the package.

They even went so far as to bring in strippers, laying us down on yoga mats while they danced on us. I'll never forget walking out of there with Connor, who turned to me, grinning ear to ear, and said, "We have to join now!"

I don't know about me, but I think Connor woke up feeling a little guilty the following day—after all, the guy did have a girlfriend. We decided to grab breakfast at the 9th Street Deli and ordered a couple of 2-foot-long subs. As we sat down to eat, Connor gave me this severe look as if he was about to drop some wisdom. But instead, what came out was a bit of a weak attempt at playing it cool. He leaned in and said, "Don't you think Delts has lost its luster?"

I could tell he was wrestling with something, but that was the moment I found my own way out of the situation, too. Without missing a beat, I shrugged and said, "Fuck it! Let's join Kap Sig." If you're not familiar with Kappa Sigma, it's that frat from my front parking lot where I first saw the picture of Dylan Grey—Julie's cousin or at least that's what I thought. Connor just looked at me, shook his head, and chuckled, "You just want to jump ship."

We both laughed, but deep down, I knew it was more than that. Later, Connor and I went to the frat to clean up after the party from the previous night. Delts didn't haze but required the pledges to clean up after parties. We had already planned on quitting the Delts, so when we walked into that room and saw the mess they had left for us to clean up, we looked at each other, thinking, "fuck this shit!" For some reason, the paper that had our names, phone numbers, and a bunch of different information about us had been left out on the counter. I picked the paper up, crossed mine and Connor's name out, wrote "too much too soon" across the paper and stuck it to the maple syrup-covered wall. Connor looked at me wide-eyed and said, "Are you trying to get us killed?" He pulled the paper back off the wall, and as we were walking out, he knocked on one of the brothers' doors and told him we no longer wanted to be in the frat. He really didn't give a shit, shrugged his shoulders and shut the door in our face. We had just officially quit the Delts.

Rambo, my former big, still wanted to be friends. I had a feeling it was mostly because he liked having access to my weed and Adderall, but I'm not going to dig into that right now. One day, he called me up and said, "I need a wingman." I was hanging out on the porch with the boys, so I stood up and told them I'd return soon. I met across campus with Rambo near some hot dog vendor by the gym.

As we munched on our hot dogs, he started telling me about the women we were about to meet. The girl he was seeing—he admitted he only hung out with her because she was a good lay and liked to buy him clothes. On the other hand, her friend needed someone to hang out with, too. I didn't say much, just nodded along, but I was definitely curious to see where this was all heading.

We finally met up with the girls, and as soon as we did, Rambo made a beeline for the one he'd been hyping up to me. Meanwhile, I figured I should at least try to be polite, so I struck up a conversation with the other girl. We talked about the usual—where I was from, my major. If you're ever trying to impress a girl in college, asking about her major is the most boring move you can make. Seriously, work on your game or pick up a magic trick or two. Anything is better than coming off like a basic dude.

Anyway, she seemed to find my newness kind of cute, and things were going smoothly. The girls clearly had a plan for everyone to get laid that night, and even though I didn't know this girl well, I was down to roll with it. At least, that was the plan—until things took a weird turn.

We headed back to the girls' place, and here's where things got dicey. They pulled out a bong and started passing it around. Now, I don't know how to explain it—maybe I'm just a magnet for disaster, or perhaps I'm too deep into the party scene—but some people just can't handle their weed. The girl I was supposed to be with took one long rip, and the next thing I knew, she was curled up on the floor, drooling like she was in a coma. Super attractive, right?

Then things got even weirder. Rambo kept insisting that he and his girl leave and that I should stay behind with this unconscious girl. Now, I might not be the sharpest tool in the shed, but I know a setup when I see one. Something didn't sit right with me. So, out of nowhere, I asked him, "Hey, do you know Cara Owens?" The way he quickly said "no" only confirmed my suspicions.

That little exchange bought me another five minutes every time. He'd try to leave, and I'd hit him with, "Do you know Cara Owens?" This back-and-forth went on for about half an hour until, finally, he blurted out, "Soccer player, small tits?"

At that moment, I saw red. If I hadn't already unleashed my rage the week before, I might've snapped and rearranged the room with his bones. Instead, I stood up, glared at him, and said, "You mean my beautiful ex-girlfriend!" Then I stormed out of there, fuming. I was angry at everyone, but honestly, I was also skinny, good-looking, vital, and young—so screw them.

As I made my dramatic exit, I couldn't help but wish that "Mr. Boombastic" was playing in the background because I looked cool as hell. Just as I reached the door, I turned back, smiled, and said, "You two should get married." With that, I stepped out, shutting the door behind me. Of course, as soon as I did, she started kissing Rambo. Typical.

As I walked away from the house, I had this odd moment of realization: somewhere along the way, I'd picked up a skinny black tie. I'm not sure how or when, but it felt like it balanced out that whole syrup-on-the-wall incident from earlier. Maybe that was my weird way of neutralizing karma. Who knows?

Chapter 14

I still made weekend trips home for work, of course, to see Julie. I would usually get calls to come home and work on significant party weekends like Homecoming. One day, my boss called to see if I could work any shifts over the weekend. I tried to play it cool, knowing this was an opportunity to see Julie. I took the last shift he offered, which was from 5 p.m. until close on Saturday.

When I got there, I walked up to Julie, trying to keep it casual. "Hi, Julie," I said, hoping for more than just a glance.

She kept her head down, smiled softly, and whispered, "Hi, Dan," before grabbing her things and heading home. It was a quick exchange, but it still felt like something. I worked the night, probably made an extra hundred bucks, and then got offered to open the next morning because "Anthony wanted an Anthony day."

Opening the shop with Julie was the highlight of my weekend. I was just excited to be around her, and I noticed right away that she had a new haircut since the last time I saw her. From about 10 feet away, I called out, "Hey, Julie, I like your shoes."

She shot back with a quick, "Dan, shut up."

I couldn't resist. "Julie, I like your shirt," I said, pushing my luck a little further.

She turned to me, half-smiling, half-annoyed, and said louder, "Dan, SHUT UP!"

But I wasn't done yet. Calmly, I added, "Julie, I like your hair." This time, she paused, fluffed her hair a bit, and smiled, but what caught my attention was the shock in her eyes as she turned to face me. It was like, for a split second, she saw me differently.

Later that day, my boss came in and asked how IUP was going. I figured he was fully informed by either Kevin or David Grey, but I played it cool and said, "It's going great. You should've seen this fight I got into." The moment those words left my mouth, everyone in the room suddenly found something fascinating on the floor, like they were in the room with a complete stranger and avoiding eye contact at all costs. It was awkward, to say the least.

Then, in my next brilliant move, I showed Julie I was dating someone. While she was pulling pizzas out of the oven, I stood about ten feet away and flashed a picture of Kylee, my new girlfriend. Julie barely glanced at it before turning away.

I'm not trying to be a tool here, but Kylee was a foreign exchange student, and we were both adults who knew what the deal was. Still, I knew it wasn't exactly a great look for me when it came to getting with Julie. But hey, you can only do so much, right?

It was now time to join Kappa Sigma, and in my mind, this was my chance to impress Julie. If you've ever made a joke of yourself, trust me, you're about to witness a masterclass.

I walked into Kappa Sigma, dragging Connor along for the ride because why not? If I was diving in, I was taking him with me. We were both interested in rushing and signing that paper. It felt like I was about to spark my destiny with the laws of physics—like somehow, this would lead to everything falling perfectly into place.

In my head, the plan was foolproof: study hard, work out, do all the frat stuff, and somehow, through the mysterious powers of the universe, it would all trickle down to Julie. They say all is fair in love and war, right? I'm not a big fan of that saying, but it sure sounded good then.

Kappa Sigma even threw a rush event that felt like it was just for Connor and me. It was on the top floor of a bar, and we met some of the brothers for the first time. I remember not seeing David Grey there, but I had heard that older brothers often skipped these events for various reasons. I wasn't about to ask about him; I didn't want to land on anyone's radar just yet.

Connor and I spent the night playing pool and shooting the breeze. Some of the brothers were still a bit hesitant about me, likely because of the fight that had gone down in their backyard the week before. But again, I was a six-foot-two, blonde-haired, blue-eyed, strong young man—what's not to like, right?

So, there it was. Kappa Sigma didn't haze. They just asked pledges to clean up after parties. Simple enough. Or so I thought.

I'm not going to sit here and pretend that being good-looking is some kind of curse. It's not—it's fantastic. So naturally, meeting beautiful women who weren't, Julie, was also on the menu. At this point, I had been rejected by Julie more times than I could count, and I had sent enough unanswered texts to finally take a hint. A guy can only bang his head against the wall for so long before he decides to look elsewhere.

Enter Elizabeth and Kayla. These two women, along with a third named Hyojung, who everyone called Korean Kylee, came into my life right before Christmas break. By that time, I had enough experience with rejection to realize it was time to make a move in a new direction. So, I did what any logical young guy would do: I started weighing my options.

But before I made any decisions, there was one particularly awkward Thanksgiving dinner that I'll never forget. In my infinite wisdom, I decided to invite all three of these women to the same dinner. Now, let me tell you, the regulars at that dinner were more than a little put off by the whole situation, but honestly, I say, screw them. It was an interesting social experiment, to say the least.

Looking back, my actions might have seemed like a seamless flow of logic at the time, but if I'm being honest, my reasoning went from conclusion to delusion pretty quickly.

So, here's what happened.

I was placed in David Grey's family within the fraternity, and guess what? I became his little's little. His little and now my big was TJ. Now, I won't go into the details of the initiation ceremony—that's for fraternity brothers only. But David was chosen to be my ultimate guide in this fraternity, which is a big deal. In the world of Kappa Sigma, a big and little relationship is supposed to be a thoughtfully crafted bond. I took that to heart.

I quickly learned that it's traditional to take your big out to lunch after the selection ceremony. I was all in for the ritual, but I didn't quite know what I was signing up for.

So, there I was, having lunch with TJ, who had presented himself as a tough, gentlemanlike guy. But things took a turn when he started calling the waitress "toots" and leering at her as she walked away. We chatted briefly about the fraternity brothers, and then, out of nowhere, he said, "I can't wait for you to meet my big, David."

Now, I had studied the faces and names of the fraternity board thoroughly. There was no other David in the frat. I tried to steer the conversation away from this unsettling comment and end the game I thought was being played on me. I hadn't slept with Korean Kylee yet—this situation could still be salvaged.

In a near-panic, I asked TJ if David was related to a girl named Julie Beachly. I analyzed his face for any sign of deceit. He seemed genuinely clueless. I thought maybe I was mistaken or that it was some higher-level conspiracy. TJ assured me he would look into any potential connection to Julie and get back to me.

A day or two later, I got a text from TJ. He assured me that his significant other, David, wasn't related to Julie and that I could finally relax. I remember looking in the mirror and feeling pretty ridiculous about the whole situation. Here I was, stressing out over a hunch and trying to piece together a connection that probably didn't even exist.

I'd joined a frat on a whim, done some cool stuff, made some great friends, and had plenty of exciting stories to share with Julie. It felt like I was finally in a place where I could breathe easily.

I wish I could say that was the end of this story. But as you might guess, things rarely wrap up neatly.

The same night I got the green light to chill out, Shrek, our resident big man, showed up at my door. He was looking to buy some Adderall and smoke some weed. My door was always open to my fraternity brothers, so we hung out for about an hour.

Then, out of nowhere, Shrek pulled out his phone and showed me a website called "The Order of the Blue Star." The site itself was nothing special, but what he said caught my attention: "TJ told me to show you this." That flipped the script on what I initially thought was just some AA-style mental rehab nonsense. At that moment, my mind went into overdrive. It felt like I could see the future, understand the past, and grasp the paradoxes we usually take for granted. I had visions of presidencies running backward to conceal the natural leader's thoughts of Mandela's effects. I ended up calling this experience "universal flight."

I know it sounds like something out of a town crier's end-of-the-world rant, but it felt like the beginning of enlightenment. I just wasn't sure how to reproduce these effects I was experiencing. At the time, I described it as psychosis, and I still believe I suffer from some degree of it. My roommate, Connor, was all too eager to point out that it was "a severe mental disorder," but logic didn't matter much to me then. I was in crunch time, trying to save the dream.

Back then, I was just a kid playing racecar, and it felt like I was in last place with an anchor dragging behind me.

Chapter 15

Life is one wild ride, isn't it? Just when you think you've got everything all figured out, the universe has a way of flipping the script. I remember feeling like I had it all under control—like I was the captain of my own ship, sailing smoothly with the world at my feet. But in all its unpredictability, life has a funny way of reminding us that we're never really in charge. One minute, you're on top of the world, and the next, you're staring at a mess you didn't even see coming. It's like trying to predict the weather in a storm—just when you think you've got a sunny forecast, the skies open up.

In this chapter, I am going to continue telling you about my wildlife to show you that it can throw curveballs, even when you think you have prepared for everything. Buckle up because this ride is about to get real.

So, let me get back to the girl who basically owned my eyes at this point and still didn't come into my life—Julie.

At this point in my life, I was texting her non-stop, asking her out, and doing everything I could to avoid hooking up with Korean Kylee. Kylee and I had agreed to wait until she got back from her trip to California so we could get to know each other better first. Or maybe she just wanted free rides to and from the airport and thought I was handsome.

Either way, I was cool with it. I mean, who knows, maybe Julie had a boyfriend—what the fuck did I know? Things were rolling along fine...

...at least until I ran into her sister.

One night, I walked into an Eat'n Park, stoned out of my mind with my boys. When my friend Ethan spotted someone, we weren't causing any trouble; we were just minding our own business.

"Hey! Isn't that Julie's sister?" He said, pointing to the booth next to ours.

Without thinking, I blurted out, "I don't like Julie. She's mean to me," completely oblivious, thanks to the weed. The second I said that line about Julie, her older sister, Diane lost it, as I'd just called Julie a cunt or thrown my ice cream in her face. She snapped—like, full-on flames-shooting-from her ears snapped. She called me every name in the book. I had ordered an ice cream, and the waiter—he could sense the weird energy at the table. He didn't even want to come near me. He literally dropped off my ice cream and kept walking, like, "Here ya go, champ," all the while she was yelling at me.

Perfect timing, right?

But I was so depressed. I was like, "I can't eat this ice cream in front of her if I ever want to face this family again."

While Diane was tearing me down in front of everyone, she said something that almost sounded like Julie might have actually had feelings for me. Or maybe it was just the way she said it. Who the hell knew at that point? Meanwhile, I'm fighting myself—my shadow self and he's got all the stamina and moves I don't.

Her shouting was so loud and angry! I just sat there staring down at my sundae, high as fuck, trying to figure out why she was so irate! Eventually I stood up and told the guys that I was with, "Let's get out of here. This isn't going well." My friends had no idea how I felt about Julie. They were just sitting there wondering why Julie's sister was being so bitchy and to be honest I was just as confused as they were.

When we were leaving, I thought about paying for her dinner, but she was with two other dudes. I was going to buy her some food to sober up, but then I thought that might insult her, you know? I didn't want to piss her off even more. Honestly, I was kind of scared of her—she was just so mad about everything.

Thinking I almost gave up on returning over Christmas break at all is diabolical. I had an interview at a movie rental place, but I turned it down once I realized it was just a winter gig. I told them I had a work family back home.

I think I was ready to tell Julie how I felt then, but she seemed unsure, and I figured it was my problem to fix. Unfortunately, being the jackass I am, I didn't pick up on the hints. At this point, I was losing my mind, still texting her every day. All I really wanted was a harsh rejection, something clear. As I write this, I feel like I'm still working on that. The day after I received the Order of the Blue Star,

I went to the frat. I walked into the main room where the boys were playing cards, thinking that together, we could make something great happen. I pulled up a chair to the head of the philanthropy board and said, "Let's cut the shit. I can make Larry president; I can make Warren a rapper—just give me the girl!"

He put his cards down, looked around the room, and said something I didn't fully understand but I got the gist of it. "You sound very condescending."

I took that to mean, "These fuckers want war." And I thought I could do war. Fuck these motherfuckers; I'm indestructible.

Oh, youth—what a plague you are.

I went back to my townhouse and replayed every detail of my relationship with Julie. I figured it was time to break things off with Kylee, but I still had to pick her up from the airport, and Julie wasn't budging, even if I sent smoke signals. I wasn't going to let fate mess with my integrity, so I picked Kylee up as promised. We went back to my place, and for the next month, we had a great time—movies, sushi, and sex. We didn't talk much, but we read books together and, yeah, had a lot of sex.

Out of all the sins I committed in this whole mess, for some reason, this relationship made me feel the guiltiest. Maybe it's because I knew deep down it could never last. Eventually, I told Julie about it—indirectly—and that's where I really fucked up. Julie used to smile whenever I was around, but the second she found out I had slept with this Korean exchange student, she never looked at me the same way again. I'll never forget the look of anger, embarrassment, and hatred in her eyes. And if you'd seen the fear inside of me at that moment, you'd know how badly I knew I'd messed up.

But really, what right did she have to be mad? We weren't dating. It seemed a bit possessive at first glance. So, she had no right to be angry with me, but she was. I don't get it—you can't reject someone a hundred times, find out they are in some shady relationship, and then be mad. You know what I mean? That's where I was coming from. And honestly, that's when I decided to declare war on everyone. And that's the beginning of how I got fired.

But then I wondered—would I have treated her the same if the roles were reversed? I mean, if she was texting me and asking me out daily, as a man, I'd need a damn good reason to turn her down.

Still, I found myself stuck in mental detention over it.

A week later, I broke up with Kylee in the most public, stupid way possible. We had a fight at a party about her wanting to stay with me over the summer, and I threw her out. I'm so fucking stupid. Never drop one without having another lined up, but I was in the market for some grand, dramatic display of love.

No one knew about my secret thing for Julie. It seemed like it was shaping up to be a home run for me—and everyone else.

So, if you're reading this and wondering if I knew all along that I had a fantastic love story in my hand, you'd be partly right. But I still had work to do. Still doing it now...

So, where are we? I guess I've just declared war on everyone at IUP—my job and anyone even slightly involved in the bullshit I'm about to unleash. By this point, I was popping Adderall to wake up and Xanax to sleep every single day.

It's February, and I'm still texting Julie. Honestly, I don't even know why. I've got everything, so why am I still messing around with this girl? She's got her eyes on me, and she's got the control. But you know what I definitely wouldn't recommend doing? Signing an agreement the day after Valentine's Day to live in a frat house the next school year. We were in the conference room of the frat signing our contracts when my phone buzzed. It was a text from Drew. It simply read, "I'm sorry to inform you, but you are fired." And like that, I no longer had a job at Fox's. Drew had always told me that even though he was the manager, he would never fire anyone because he felt like that was the owner's responsibility, but this time was different. He made it a point to be the one who told me I was fired because we were friends, and I respected that. When I told Connor about it, he said, "I'd be pissed as fuck." I just shrugged and said, "Nah," all while sitting at my dealer Ranger Stone's place, smoking a ridiculous amount of weed.

Chapter 16

Before I dive deeper into the meltdown and the chaos that followed, you need to understand the kind of mind the guys I had in my life had. This wasn't just some college kid burning the candle at both ends—no, this was a full-blown mental battlefield. I was living in a haze of Adderall-fueled highs and Xanax-induced lows, walking a tightrope between ambition and self-destruction. It's hard to explain, but everything feels urgent, dramatic, and somehow justified when you're in that state.

I wasn't just reacting to the world around me; I was creating my own chaos. And honestly? I kind of enjoyed it. The intensity, the recklessness, the "fuck you" attitude—it all felt like a badge of honor. Like I was fighting for something, even if I couldn't tell you what it was. So yeah, this chapter is for the boys who were right there in the trenches with me, either hyping me up or watching me burn.

I was known for my eccentricities, which you'll fully grasp by the end of this book. One perfect example? The Madden tournament at my place. Out of eight people, I somehow made it to the championship, facing off against the frat president himself. It was Madden 13, with Calvin Johnson on the cover. I picked the Minnesota Vikings because of Adrian Peterson, and he went with the Detroit Lions for Calvin Johnson.

The game was absolutely insane! We had phenomenal picks, crazy stops, and clutch moments that had everyone on edge. The atmosphere was electric! Guys from the frat I barely knew and my boys from high school were all huddled around, watching every move, cheering, and heckling like we were playing in the Super Bowl.

I could go on and on about this game, but it all came down to me getting cocky and scoring in just three plays.

"You got nothing on my three plays!" I shouted. To this motherfucker's credit, immediately after those words left my mouth, he turned around and scored a touchdown in two plays. He looked at me dead in the eye and said, "How about my two plays?"

At that point, I was backed into a corner and didn't want to risk overtime. I remembered from an old Madden trick that if I timed it right, I could jump the snap and block the extra point. In theory, I had to hit the edge at the perfect moment and block the ball. So, I focused, listened to the clicks of his controller, and when I thought it was time—I went for it.

Boom! I blocked the extra point, and the entire room erupted! I swear, the way they acted, you'd think I had performed a real-life miracle. One of the brothers was literally hyperventilating, yelling, "I can't believe you did that! I CAN'T BELIEVE IT!" I just sat there, grinning, about as happy as I could be.

That moment? Probably my second favorite story of all time.

Chapter 17

As the days passed, I went into a full-on craze over watching the news. I started reading stuff like *Mein Kampf* and *How to Teach Your Dogs Physics* (because those two totally intersect) and diving into conspiracy theories about how we're all being propagandized. I wanted to understand the most messed up guy in the world, the most strait-laced guy, and everyone in between. And honestly, I always felt like that guy in the middle. Like, I smoked just enough weed to be somewhere in between all that chaos, you know what I mean?

I'd watch the news, and if it didn't fit my view, I figured it was fake, but if it aligned with my thinking, I assumed it was real. This eventually warped into some seriously dark shit. Everything started to feel off—like job titles had hidden meanings, and time itself didn't make sense, like we had all done this before, and I was the first one to remember it. I was deep in psychosis, and part of me recognized it as something special but also extremely dangerous.

At this point, I was smoking enough weed to subdue Genghis Khan's entire army, trying to keep myself grounded. I'd love to say that was the end of my adventures with other women, but *nope*.

Elizabeth was my neighbor, so I saw her daily, and Kayla always hung around the frat. I was only sleeping with about fifty percent of them, but still—this wasn't leading to a good ending, and honestly, I was beginning to care less and less about the outcome.

I stayed holed up in my room, losing my mind, until about St. Patrick's Day. When I finally emerged outside, I literally had a run-in with Julie. I'd just stepped out onto my porch when Julie walked out of Elizabeth's apartment, sporting a green IUPatties shirt. I got right up in her face, but she didn't flinch. It was pretty clear she was trying to end things, but honestly, in that moment, I was more determined to show her who I really was than to accept a simple ending.

So, I let her go. I walked straight over to Elizabeth's place, ending things with her and demanding to know if a girl with brown hair was in her apartment. She said yeah, Julie was here. I asked what had been said, and she replied, "She didn't say much."

Fucking bitches. Either way, it was officially over with Elizabeth.

My next step was a bit more methodical and thought out. I decided to get my pledge paddle back from my big in my fraternity, TJ, and turn it into a beacon. Before I get into it, please seek me out for what I owe you—not just the paddle but the inspiration behind the cover of this novel. Sweet girl, she took Adderall to draw me the picture from high school that led me to Julie on my paddle.

Anyway, after my paddle was complete, I went back to TJ and presented it to him in front of our class president, telling him it was something that had followed me around in high school. I was hoping to pass the message down the chain of command.

When you make moves like this, you hope for immediate results, but that's rarely how it works when others are strategizing against you. But I digress.

I went through even more stages of psychosis. I felt like the devil incarnate, but with one big difference: I was convinced I was destined to create a story more powerful than the Bible. And don't get it twisted—before you think I'm like the Beatles claiming to be bigger than Jesus, I said more powerful. I honestly believe Fight Club has a better storyline than the Bible. That's just my take, though. Yours can be different.

At this point, the frat brothers were just messing with me. I finally had my chance to meet David Grey during alumni night, and I will admit, I was scared shitless. I wasn't worried he'd kick my ass himself, but I feared a whole squad of motherfuckers coming after me. You never really know how your actions affect people until you talk it out, and some folks are like Helen Keller in this shit; deaf and blind.

So, I met David's friends, who recognized me as his little's little right off the bat. It was pretty unsettling. They pushed me up the stairs, leading me to him. When I stepped into the room, finally coming face to face with David, I threw my arm around him like I was ready to put him in a headlock and choke him out while they stomped me. But it went well. We shook hands and talked for a bit about sports.

Then TJ took me, David, and a few girls to his room. He pulled out a six-pack of expensive beer and handed one to each of us, even saying, "They're better warm." I mean, fuck, I've eaten raw meatballs for the sake of keeping the brothers' girlfriends happy. What was a warm beer!?

Then, some girl started rubbing my leg and flirting with me. I lifted her hand off my leg and said I have a girlfriend (referring to my uncertain romance with Julie). David's eyes shifted to me, and he smiled knowingly.

Eventually, we left the room and headed into the kitchen, where they were doing the chug chant. Want to guess who got chosen to chug and what name they used for him? You guessed it! It was David, and they called him Brother Gregory. I stared into his eyes, feeling both excited and pissed off, chanting "Brother Gregory!" with everyone else as he lifted his beer and chugged it.

It was a full-blown war now.

What I did next, I'll never truly understand. I felt like I needed to retaliate after the Brother Gregory thing. That first night, I played the role of Romeo, delivering a note by the standards of Romeo and Juliet. I showed up with a bagged lunch containing a cryptic note inside that read, "I don't know what dating is; I'm sorry if I cheated on you while we were dating." The bag held a good steak, an apple, and the folded-up note with an asterisk on the front.

I then argued with my male boss, insisting he deliver the bag to Julie. We went back and forth over it, and I think his curiosity got the best of him. He asked, "Are you messing with me?" and I yelled, "You're just an asterisk!"

The next day, I was at my friend Ethan's house, losing my mind trying to explain the situation, but he didn't believe me. So, we ordered 12 breadsticks and a 2L of Sierra Mist at Fox's Pizza. For scientific purposes, of course.

Oddly, we got a call back from Julie's best friend, who said, "I can't deliver that order."

I said, "Well, you tell your people, and I'll tell mine, and we'll get our papers together and go from there."

She said *OKAY*, and we hung up.

Later, Ethan and I decided to hit Sheetz for some food and pop. When we got back to my car, I noticed the note I had put in the bag the night before was on the passenger side floor. When I looked at it and asked Ethan, "Who put this here?" he replied, "Uh, you did." Because he's a fake fucking friend.

Then some serious shit happened. I lost it like Britney Spears. One night, I went to my apartment at IUP, got drunk and high, and that's when the cathead people started talking to me.

Here's a side note: I picked up a cat because Julie told me to after I mentioned that my cat, Charlie Sheen, had died. I wanted a new cat and asked if she wanted me to bring it by. She said yes, so I figured I was getting a new cat. I spent the last forty bucks in my wallet on kitten supplies and brought everything back. When I showed it to her, she just shrugged!

Anyway, back to the talking cats on TV. It was Adult Swim on Cartoon Network, and they were about to air an episode of *American Dad* that would mess with me internally for a long time. The episode was called "The Boring Identity." In it, Stan, the father, and CIA agent, had to take out the real Bin Laden. And, of all things, my name was penciled in on Bin Laden's name tag. Not to mention the cantaloupe and watermelon scene that opened the episode—I guess I was a cantaloupe.

So, Stan takes out Bin Laden and all the coworkers at a Buster Fuckers or some Dave & Buster's knockoff. Then, Stan hops on a video game motorcycle and takes it to "downtown Tokyo," which I took as a metaphor for dating the Korean girl. He then flies off the bike and hits his head, losing his memory, which I saw as me losing my mind. His boss, Bullock, even lost his mind, as I had imagined all my friends would. "Somebody call somebody"—oh, if only.

I then texted the group chat, begging for help. I pled with them to stop the war and offered my expertise for the second time. I was invited to the frat president's home and had a bed made up for me. I've never felt so welcomed and yet so insulted when they told me to calm down and that they had no idea what I was talking about. But I was talking to the TV, so touché.

You might think that this book is full of dark shit, but it isn't even over yet, so hold on to your seatbelts, folks!

Coming back to the story, I began drinking heavier, smoking more weed, and mixing in Adderall and Xanax. Although it made me feel stable, I knew deep down it was only because I was nineteen and in great shape. I was caught between madness and enlightenment. One moment, I could walk through the courtyard and compliment everyone I passed; the next, I couldn't make it out of the house without thinking about wearing a cape. But that's mania, I suppose.

The original paddle I had presented to TJ was just some thrown-together homemade thing I had done on a whim, so I decided to have another one that was much nicer and more thought out. When I finally picked up my newly finished pledge paddle, I showed it to TJ and decided at the last minute that I wanted something extra on the back. What I had written isn't even necessary. But what is essential is that on the drive home, out of nowhere, this dark thought crept in, and like I had no control, I just let it take over. The next thing I know, I'm rolling right into traffic as if I were some secret agent triggered by a code word.

It all happened so fast. I swerved at the last second, barely avoiding a T-bone crash. Both cars got scratched up, but it could've been way worse. And I remember just sitting there, trying to figure out—*was that an accident? Or was I actually trying to end it?*

The next thing I knew, it was April. I had given up on every woman I was sexually or emotionally involved with. I withdrew from my college classes and hunkered down in my room, with my only trips being to the frat house. That's where they got me. My second-to-last fuckup with Juie, but undoubtedly the final nail in the coffin.

I was drinking one night when I glanced at Connor's girlfriend's phone and saw "Melissa down." I figured it was code because the last time I saw Melissa, we were eating tacos on Connor's bed. Maybe I was paranoid, but I remember saying, "Julie is coming tonight," and Kristen said, "You can just feel it, huh?" I then grabbed a glass of Jack Daniels and chugged it with Dr. Pepper. A glass doesn't do it justice—it was a gauntlet of whiskey.

I then ventured out on my own. I went through the downstairs of the house and up the back steps, trying to throw off anyone who might be watching. Stupid move. I was looking for her—what did it matter how we ran into each other? I went up the stairs, under the bar, and checked the scene where I thought she might be. But I was wrong. I decided to check downstairs, figuring she might be in the lounge, maybe playing Super Smash Brothers with the boys. What did I know?

As I went down the stairs, I walked by three girls without even turning my head. When I got to the fourth, without even thinking, I turned my whole body, shocked instantly by the resemblance, and asked, "Do you know Julie Beachley?" She responded by putting both hands on her chest and yelling, "I'M JULIE!" Scared the hell out of me. I should have kissed her then, but I froze up, head tilted sideways, and said, "Tell her I said I miss her," like the demon was coming back through my vocal cords. She nodded three times. I darted to each of her friends, saying, "Tell her I said I miss her," to each one before reversing course and heading back up the stairs I'd just come down. When I got to the top, a brother grabbed me and yelled, "IF YOU NEED ANYTHING!" I laughed insatiably, fearlessly scared. I immediately knew what I had to do: sober up.

I went back the way I came and exited the building. I walked around the corner and up the street to a local place called Pita Pit. To this day, I don't remember a more satisfying, tasty meal. I even did something I don't usually do—littered as I walked in because I was on a fucking mission and didn't give a damn about anyone else.

I walked back in, retracing my steps through the same route I'd taken earlier, and found her in the scene room. It was the place where beer pong and social politics were discussed. I approached her from behind, tapped her shoulder, and asked, "Do you know Julie Beachley?" This time, she was visibly annoyed. She pointed at herself and snapped, "I'M JULIE!"

I threw up my hands and casually said, like it was my catchphrase, "Tell her I said I miss her." I then made my way to the dance floor and jumped up on some furniture. The details of what happened next are a blur. I moved around and danced, and the only thing I remember clearly was my mind with Julie. The song playing was "Turn Down for What" by DJ Snake and Lil Jon. If you know the song, you know it's not a slow dance melody.

Something about that night transformed the dance floor. I was right at the front, as close to the speakers as possible. I didn't even notice someone next to me until I felt the smoothness of her arm as I ran my hand down it. When the beat dropped, I jumped to the left, my hand gliding along her arm in a sweeping motion. We stayed like that throughout the entire drop; all I could focus on was the connection of our hands.

I walked away, laughing, knowing I'd probably caused more damage than good.

I stepped outside for a cigarette and saw her walking past me alone, looking like she'd seen a ghost. All I did was wave and say, "Tell her I said I miss her." After she walked away, I did too. Julie never attended prom, so I always hoped that night did something for her.

The next day was a letdown. I waited for a text or some sign, but when I asked my roommate Connor if Julie was there last night, he snapped, "NO!" I tried to explain, but he cut me off, saying, "I don't know who was here, but you scared the fuck out of them."

I went outside, where I saw a frat brother smoking a cigarette. When I approached him, he started to tremble. I told him that if Julie came back, we needed to make a plan. He responded, "Well, we'll cross that bridge when we come to it." I was thrown off by his response but figured it was coming to an end. I just needed to think of the perfect ending.

Chapter 18

There is one more story I would like to share with you before the end of this book. It's pretty amusing, actually. Well, at the moment, it wasn't funny, but now I can look back and laugh. So here it goes. I got mugged twice in one night by the same dude. Yes, you read that correctly. I was mugged twice in one night by the same guy! Let me explain. My memory from that night is a bit hazy, but this is how it happened.

My buddy Lou hit me up the next day after my encounter with Julie at the frat and said to me, "Hey man, I know you're losing your mind. You should come home!" Followed by what I assumed his actual intention behind the invitation was. His following text read, "Could you do me a favor? Can you drive my girlfriend to Whitefield?" Whitefield was a four-hour drive for me, but I didn't really have anything else going on, so I figured why not.

I responded with, "Hey, anything for you, buddy." And with that, the adventure began. When we finally got to Lou's place, we hung out for a bit before heading out to a party.

Whitefield is known for being a rough neighborhood, but I thought we could handle it ourselves. Deep down, I was still upset that I hadn't heard anything from Julie since last night. What a fucking mess this whole thing had become. Who knows, maybe going out and partying would help take my mind off the turmoil that was going on inside me.

We get to the party, start drinking, and just having a good time. After a little while, Lou says he is going to introduce his girlfriend to some of his friends so they can enjoy the party and that he will find me again later. As he walked away with her, he gave me a nod, which apparently meant, "Don't leave the party."

But I was feeling adventurous and invincible, so I thought, Screw it. I walked around and eventually met some girls who asked if I wanted to party with them. Who was I to tell these girls? No, so I followed them. They kept leading me to different parties. Truth be told, I was having a great time, so I didn't mind. At one point, I even ended up at a laundry mat, sitting and talking with one of the girls while she did her laundry. After that brief intermission, her laundry was done, and she led me to another party, where, you guessed it, I met more girls. I tagged along with them all night until, eventually, they all headed home. I suddenly realized I had no idea where I was anymore, so I just started wandering around, trying to get back to where I originally started.

As I was walking down the sidewalk, this random dude across the street raised his hand, waving at me and yelling, "Hey man, you like bitches and drugs..."

I immediately shot back, "I love bitches and drugs," matching his enthusiasm. "Then follow me!" he shouted, and with that, I crossed the street, following him to what I assumed would be one hell of a good party.

This, however, is when things started to go south. We were walking and talking when suddenly I felt this burst of air go by my face, followed by a punch to the back of the head. I don't think I have ever been punched so hard. I hit the ground and put my arm up, instinctually trying to protect myself from whatever came next. But nothing happened.

I jumped up and looked around, trying to figure out who had just hit me. The guy I was just with had turned around and started walking quickly in the opposite direction from where I was, presumingly trying not to be the next victim. I jogged back up to him, asking him if he had seen who had jumped us. He just looked at me with these big, bulging eyes like, "Uh, are you serious?" We kept walking while I rambled on about how we needed to find the fucker that hit me and took my wallet.

But... after about ten steps from where we were, I felt that familiar breeze on my face, and *he hit me again.* That's right. I was so intoxicated it never dawned on me that the guy I had been walking with was the one who had actually mugged me. This time, when I hit the ground, he took what was in my front pockets and sprinted off. I lay there for a moment, trying to wrap my head around what had just happened.

When I finally got up, I looked around, realizing I was still lost. My party was on Fourth Street, but when I looked around, all I saw were street signs that read Christmas Tree and Campbell. When did the streets with numbers end? I thought as if the reality of the situation hit me. I continued wandering around for what seemed like forever until I finally approached a group of people sitting on their front porch. I was desperate and really didn't have much else to lose. "Hey man, I got jumped twice. I have no phone, no money, and no idea where I am. Can you please just give me a ride back to Fourth Street?" I said to the guy standing closest to me.

They all looked at each other and laughed. One of the guys finally composed himself enough to say, "Sure, we will take you, but you're riding up front." I was nervous for a moment, but then I realized the girl in the group was the one driving. I doubt they would kill me with her in the car, right? I was so thankful for them giving me a ride. I kept promising them that if they came to IUP, I would get them into any party they wanted.

They dropped me off, and I stumbled back into the party where I was supposed to be. I found Lou and frantically told him how I had been mugged. He just looked at me like I was the luckiest guy on earth. Apparently, that was a common initiation for new gang members in the area. I was fortunate to be alive.

Chapter 19

We are finally on the last chapter of this depraved recklessness of a book. It is the final point where I tell you how my life spiraled, twisted, and turned into unfavorable outcomes—all of which I deserved (you can surely understand why).

At this point, all that was keeping me going was a plan to walk up to Julie, admit my feelings, and figure it out from there. The first time I tried talking to her at work, I stood over her while she stocked bread. Instead of telling her how I felt, I just simply demanded, blurting out, "I want to talk to you." She replied, "I don't want to talk," and I left.

The second time I walked into Fox's, my great friend Maddison told me, "You're not allowed to be here," so I walked out. But then I turned around, walked back in, and said, "I'm a customer," pointing at myself. Maddison shot back with, "Hey, it's not me." As I went to leave the shop, I noticed Julie pull out her phone as I left. When I got home, a cop was waiting in my driveway. He told me, "No one wants to press charges; she just doesn't want you in that pizza shop."

That infuriated me! I jumped up and down, yelling at the cop, "Nelson Mandela spent 27 years in jail for love!" or some crazy shit like that and stormed off.

The third time was odd. I decided to try offering a peace treaty, and I think she was trying to do the same. I walked into the pizza shop holding my frat hoodie, the one given to me by my big. Julie walked out the back, and instead of following her as I should have, I handed my hoodie to the manager, saying, "I found this at a party. I think it's her boyfriend's." The manager took it, so that was a bust.

The fourth and final time, I decided I wasn't leaving, even if the cops showed up. She was acting eccentric, and it was messing with my emotions like crazy! I didn't even know what gaslighting was back then.

It was so weird. I walked in, took off my Ray-Ban glasses, and put them on the table next to Maddison. I told her, "Tell Julie to give Cara back her glasses." Maddison looked at me and said, "Danny, I thought you were wearing them."

Julie then walked into the office and closed the door. I tried to get my "friends" to help me out and get her, but no one moved. So, I went outside to wait for the cops to show up. For some reason, my friend Ethan was there, and he fucking bolted when he saw the cops pull up.

I went back inside to grab my glasses and ran straight into the cops. They had more cop cars there than I'd seen at my own mother's suicide attempt, and the Dairy Queen drive-through line next door was packed with vehicles watching me get arrested. I took it well, even managing to smile at a girl I went to high school with. I mean, in my head, I was just playing the role.

I wasn't in cuffs until this elderly cop got a radio call. The next thing I knew, he said, "Son, this is for my safety." I kind of trusted I could take him even with the cuffs on. Then my boss showed up with papers saying I was fired and that people who are fired are not allowed on the premises.

I was charged with trespassing, and that was it. The cops that took me to the station were surprisingly lovely and told me I would have to pay a fine or go to court and appeal my case. I will admit, I kept trying to break out of my cuffs as a joke. I didn't really take the moment seriously.

Let me explain a bit. Remember how I said the TV would talk to me sometimes? Well, I got over the thought that the TV was speaking directly to me, but it certainly wasn't crazy to say that it influenced me. The night before I went into the pizza shop for the last time, I watched two movies: *Pulp Fiction* and *Anger Management* with Adam Sandler. I'm not even going to try to explain how they affected me—just go watch the damn movies.

Anyway, knowing this whole mess needed an ending, I was ready for a long, serious talk. Then my parents showed up, lecturing me about needing rehab for drugs and all that. But the best part? The cop who'd been so lovely to me walked over and handed me my glasses—except the left arm of it was bent into a perfect uppercase L, like a 90-degree angle.

I took it as a challenge. Do you know how those cheesy romance movies always end with someone running through an airport? I decided to adapt and survive. I handed my mom the glasses and took them off inside. I reached the door, glanced back at my dad and the cops—all with different expressions on their faces—and then I ran back into the pizza shop, screaming, "Why the fuck did you bend my glasses?" As I sprinted, I noticed the once-clear back exit was now blocked off. Maddison threw out her arms and shouted, "Dan, stop!" I skidded to a halt right there.

That moment was seared into my memory—every detail, from the smell to the surreal feeling of divine observation (or maybe it was just the weed). With my eyes glued to the ground, I rolled my head up to the right, hoping Julie might come out of the office. She didn't. I looked up at the ceiling, half-expecting some divine intervention to pluck me from the commotion surrounding me. No such luck.

Then, I turned around slowly, my face breaking into an insane grin. Two cops were hot on my tail. And as I reflected on their response time, I thought, "I could've destroyed this entire building before they even got in." If the exit hadn't been blocked, I might still be outrunning them like Forest Gump. But, as always, I fucking digress.

When they caught up to me, I was tackled and put into handcuffs after putting up a lazy ass fight. I was charged with stalking and resisting arrest. Five days later, I had my hearing, and I finally got home.

That summer was rough. I was left feeling shattered and indecisive about returning to IUP. I was so broken that I fantasized about showing up with a bat, a shovel, and a revenge plan. But instead, I decided to create a Twitter handle: "Campus Scientist." It seemed like a last-ditch effort to reclaim some semblance of normalcy. I figured, why not reach out to Julie, and ask to be friends? After all, I had her number but never made a move to connect with her on Twitter.

It took a while, but eventually, she unlocked her profile to the public and then locked it again. During that brief window, I saw a few things—some cryptic posts that might have been about me, but one post was painfully clear. It read, "I wish I was half as interesting as my stalker thinks," followed by comments from her friends laughing about the trouble I'd gotten into. It felt like a punch to the gut. The mockery stung deeply, especially since she never reached out or called.

In her book, I had become a stalker. What a perfect way to end this chaotic book...

Conclusion

This book is a way for me to help process my emotions surrounding the events that transpired as well as all the trouble I caused for everyone around me, including my oldest pal, Dan Edmunds Jr. Any sane reader who read this book would understand that I was a jerk—a full-blown one. Come on, you don't have to sugarcoat or say, "No, Dan! Bad things happened to you, and you turned out this way!" Well, to an extent, that may be true, but I sincerely believe that the decisions I made in my life were all on me—my upbringing and constant turmoil with my monster of a big brother were just added backdrops.

Like, let's retake a look: I cheated on girls, I played with their feelings, I got into fights, I dealt with weed and alcohol, I was a frat member (frat members are rarely decent, we all know that), and I got into many more deceitful and uncivil shenanigans. True, I did have my positives—like giving my many girlfriends the attention they wanted, listening to people and helping them, standing up for myself against my brother and my enemies, and most of all—being a loyal friend to my brothers.

Still, this does not, in any way, dwindle the negatives, and I wrote this book to accept that and move on—and also give you an exciting story to pass the time.

Now, I cannot end this book without addressing some people. There are three levels to that:

First, to my frat brothers: *run from me*. I swear to God, if I catch you, it's on sight. You better believe it.

Second, to the cops who bent my glasses—we're good! I don't hold grudges.

Third, to the one and only—Julie. Look, I am exhausted at this point. Is this interesting enough for you?

As a parting thought, listen up, everyone. I am sorry I didn't play the role everyone thought I would. I had a car and good intentions. I am sorry your emotions weren't part of the contingency plan, but sometimes Batman has a genuine love interest. And sometimes he knows when it's too much, too soon. I don't know where to go from here, but I'm done living in the past.

With love,

The Campus Scientist

Suicide does not stop the hurt. It simply passes the pain on to the ones you leave behind.

No matter how bad the situation or how alone you feel, you can make it through with the right help and support.

Help is always available by calling the National Suicide Prevention Lifeline.

1-800-273-8255

This is a free 24/7 hotline to help anyone in a suicidal crisis or emotional distress!